Thomas Nelson Page

Santa Claus' Partner

Thomas Nelson Page

Santa Claus' Partner

ISBN/EAN: 9783744660433

Printed in Europe, USA, Canada, Australia, Japan

Cover: Foto ©Thomas Meinert / pixelio.de

More available books at **www.hansebooks.com**

SANTA CLAUS'S
PARTNER

BY

THOMAS NELSON PAGE

ILLUSTRATED BY W. GLACKENS

NEW YORK
CHARLES SCRIBNER'S SONS
1899

TO MY FATHER

who among all the men the writer knew ... ...s youth was the most familiar with books ; and who of all the men the writer has ever known has exemplified best the virtue of open-handedness, this little Book is affectionately inscribed by his son,

THE AUTHOR

ILLUSTRATIONS

FROM DRAWINGS IN COLOR BY W. GLACKENS

SANTA CLAUS'S PARTNER

CHAPTER I

BERRYMAN LIVINGSTONE was a successful man, a very successful man, and as he sat in his cushioned chair in his inner private office (in the best office-building in the city) on a particularly snowy evening in December, he looked it every inch. It spoke in every line of his clean-cut, self-contained face, with its straight, thin nose, closely drawn mouth, strong chin and clear gray eyes; in every movement of his erect, trim, well-groomed figure; in every detail of his faultless attire; in every tone of his assured, assertive, incisive speech. As some one said of him, he always looked as if he had just been ironed.

[1]

He used to be spoken of as "a man of parts;" now he was spoken of as "a man of wealth — a capitalist."

Not that he was as successful as he intended to be; but the way was all clear and shining before him now. It was now simply a matter of time. He could no more help going on to further heights of success than his "gilt-edged" securities, stored in thick parcels in his safe-deposit boxes, could help bearing interest.

He contemplated the situation this snowy evening with a deep serenity that brought a transient gleam of light to his somewhat cold face.

He knew he was successful by the silent envy with which his acquaintances regarded him; by the respect with which he was treated and his opinion was received at the different Boards, of which he was now an influential member, by men who fifteen years

[2]

ago hardly knew of his existence. He knew it by the numbers of invitations to the most fashionable houses which crowded his library table; by the familiar and jovial air with which presidents and magnates of big corporations, who could on a moment's notice change from warmth—temperate warmth—to ice, greeted him; and by the cajoling speeches with which fashionable mammas with unmarried daughters of a certain or uncertain age rallied him about his big, empty house on a fashionable street, and his handsome dinners, where only one thing was wanting—the thing they had in mind.

Berryman Livingstone had, however, much better proof of success than the mere plaudits of the world. Many men had these who had no real foundation for their display. For instance, "Meteor" Broome the broker, had just taken the big house on the corner above him, and had filled his stable with high-step-

[3]

ping, high-priced horses—much talked of in
the public prints—and his wife wore jewels
as handsome as Mrs. Parke-Rhode's who
owned the house and twenty more like it.
Colonel Keightly was one of the largest
dealers on 'Change this year and was adver-
tised in all the papers as having made a cool
million and a half in a single venture out
West. Van Diver was always spoken of as
the "Grain King," "Mining King," or some
other kind of Royalty, because of his infallible
success, and Midan touch.

But though these and many more like them
were said to have made in a year or two more
than Livingstone with all his pains had been
able to accumulate in a score of years of earnest toil and assiduous devotion to business;
were now invited to the same big houses
that Livingstone visited, and were greeted by
almost as flattering speeches as Livingstone
received, Livingstone knew of discussions as

[4]

to these men at Boards other than the "festal
board," and of "stiffer" notes that had been
sent them than those stiff and sealed missives
which were left at their front doors by liver-
ied footmen.

Livingstone, however, though he "kept out
of the papers," having a rooted and growing
prejudice against this form of vulgarity, could
at any time, on five minutes' notice, establish
the solidity of his foundation by simply un-
locking his safe-deposit boxes. His foundation
was as solid as gold.

On the mahogany table-desk before him lay
now a couple of books : one a long, ledger-like
folio in the russet covering sacred to the bind-
ing of that particular kind of work which a
summer-hearted Writer of books years ago
inscribed as "a book of great interest ;" the
other, a smaller volume, a memorandum book,
more richly attired than its sober companion,
in Russia leather.

[5]

For an hour or two Mr. Livingstone, with closely-drawn, thin lips, and eager eyes, had sat in his seat, silent, immersed, absorbed, and compared the two volumes, from time to time making memoranda in the smaller book, whilst his clerks had sat on their high stools in the large office outside looking impatiently at the white-faced clock on the wall as it slowly marked the passing time, or gazing enviously and grumblingly out of the windows at the dark, hurrying crowds below making their way homeward through the falling snow.

The young men could not have stood it but for the imperturbable patience and sweet temper of the oldest man in the office, a quiet-faced, middle-aged man, who, in a low, cheery, pleasant voice, restrained their impatience and soothed their ruffled spirits.

Even this, however, was only partially successful.

"Go in there, Mr. Clark, and tell him we

want to go home," urged fretfully one youth, a tentative dandy, with a sharp nose and blunt chin, who had been diligently arranging his vivid necktie for more than a half-hour at a little mirror on the wall.

"Oh! He'll be out directly now," replied the older man, looking up from the account-book before him.

"You've been saying that for three hours!" complained the other.

"Well, see if it doesn't come true this time," said the older clerk, kindly. "He'll make it up to you."

This view of the case did not seem to appeal very strongly to the young man; he simply grunted.

"I'm going to give him notice. I'll not be put upon this way—" bristled a yet younger clerk, stepping down from his high stool in a corner and squaring his shoulders with martial manifestations.

[7]

This unexpected interposition appeared to be the outlet the older grumbler wanted.

"Yes, you will!" he sneered with disdain, turning his eyes on his junior derisively. He could at least bully Sipkins.

For response, the youngster walked with a firm tread straight up to the door of the private office; put out his hand so quickly that the other's eyes opened wide; then turned so suddenly as to catch his derider's look of wonder; stuck out his tongue in triumph at the success of his ruse, and walked on to the window.

"He'll be through directly, see if he is not," reiterated the senior clerk with kindly intonation. "Don't make a noise, there's a good fellow;" and once more John Clark, the dean of the office, guilefully buried himself in his columns.

"He must be writing his love-letters. Go in there, Hartley, and help him out. You're an

[8]

adept at that," hazarded the youngster at the window to the dapper youth at the mirror.

There was a subdued explosion from all the others but Clark, after which, as if relieved by this escape of steam, the young men quieted down, and once more applied themselves to looking moodily out of the windows, whilst the older clerk gave a secret peep at his watch, and then, after another glance at the closed door of the private office, went back once more to his work.

Meantime, within his closed sanctum Livingstone still sat with intent gaze, poring over the page of figures before him. The expression on his face was one of profound satisfaction. He had at last reached the acme of his ambition—that is, of his later ambition. (He had once had other aims.) He had arrived at the point towards which he had been straining for the last eight—ten—fifteen years—he did not try to remember just how long—it

[9]

had been a good while. He had at length accumulated, "on the most conservative estimate" (he framed the phrase in his mind, following the habit of his Boards)—he had no need to look now at the page before him: the seven figures that formed the balance, as he thought of them, suddenly appeared before him in facsimile. He had been gazing at them so steadily that now even when he shut his eyes he could see them clearly. It gave him a little glow about his heart;—it was quite convenient: he could always see them.

It was a great sum. He had attained his ambition.

Last year when he balanced his books at the close of the year, he had been worth only —a sum expressed in six figures, even when he put his securities at their full value. Now it could only be written in seven figures, "on the most conservative estimate."

Yes, he had reached the top. He could walk

up the street now and look any man in the face, or turn his back on him, just as he chose. The thought pleased him.

Years ago, a friend—an old friend of his youth, Harry Trelane, had asked him to come down to the country to visit him and meet his children and see the peach trees bloom. He had pleaded business, and his friend had asked him gravely why he kept on working so hard when he was already so well off. He wanted to be rich, he had replied.

"But you are already rich—you must be worth half a million? and you are a single man, with no children to leave it to."

" Yes, but I mean to be worth double that."

"Why?"

"Oh!—so that I can tell any man I choose to go to the d—l," he had said half jestingly, being rather put to it by his friend's earnestness. His friend had laughed too, he remembered, but not heartily.

[11]

"Well, that is not much of a satisfaction after all," he had said; "the real satisfaction is in helping him the other way;"—and this Livingstone remembered he had said very earnestly.

Livingstone now had reached this point of his aspiration—he could tell any man he chose "to go to the devil."

His content over this reflection was shadowed only by a momentary recollection that Henry Trelane was since dead. He regretted that his friend could not know of his success.

Another friend suddenly floated into his memory. Catherine Trelane was his collegemate's sister. Once she had been all the world to Livingstone, and he had found out afterwards that she had cared for him too, and would have married him had he spoken at one time. But he had not known this at first, and when he began to grow he could not bring himself to it. He could not afford

to burden himself with a family that might
interfere with his success. Then later, when
he had succeeded and was well off and had
asked Catherine Trelane to be his wife, she
had declined. She said Livingstone had not offered her himself, but his fortune. It had stung
Livingstone deeply, and he had awakened,
but too late, to find for a while that he had
really loved her. She was well off too, having
been left a comfortable sum by a relative.

However, Livingstone was glad now, as he
reflected on it, that it had turned out so.
Catherine Trelane's refusal had really been
the incentive which had spurred him on to
greater success. It was to revenge himself that
he had plunged deeper into business than
ever, and he had bought his fine house to
show that he could afford to live in style.
He had intended then to marry; but he had
not had time to do so; he had always been
too busy.

SANTA CLAUS'S PARTNER

Catherine Trelane, at least, was not dead. He had not heard of her in a long time; she had married, he knew, a man named — Shepherd, he believed, and he had heard that her husband was dead.

He would see that she knew he was worth —the page of figures suddenly flashed in before his eyes like a magic-lantern slide. Yes, he was worth all that! and he could now marry whom and when he pleased.

CHAPTER II

LIVINGSTONE closed his books. He had put everything in such shape that Clark, his confidential clerk, would not have the least trouble this year in transferring everything and starting the new books that would now be necessary.

Last year Clark had been at his house a good many nights writing up these private books; but that was because Clark had been in a sort of muddle last winter,—his wife was sick, or one of his dozen children had met with an accident,— or something,— Livingstone vaguely remembered.

This year there would be no such trouble. Livingstone was pleased at the thought; for Clark was a good fellow, and a capable book-keeper, even though he was a trifle slow.

Livingstone felt that he had, in a way, a high regard for Clark. He was attentive to

[15]

his duties, beyond words. He was a gentleman, too,—of a first-rate family—a man of
principle. How he could ever have been content to remain a simple clerk all these years,
Livingstone could not understand. It gave
him a certain contempt for him. That came,
he reflected, of a man's marrying indiscreetly
and having a houseful of children on his back.

Clark would be pleased at the showing on
the books. He was always delighted when the
balances showed a marked increase.

Livingstone was glad now that he had not
only paid the old clerk extra for his night-
work last year, but had given him fifty dollars additional, partly because of the trouble
in his family, and partly because Livingstone
had been unusually irritated when Clark got
the two accounts confused.

Livingstone prided himself on his manner
to his employees. He prided himself on being
a gentleman, and it was a mark of a gen-

tleman always to treat subordinates with ci-
vility. He knew men in the city who were
absolute bears to their employees; but they
were blackguards.

He, perhaps, ought to have discharged
Clark without a word; that would have been
"business;" but really he ought not to have
spoken to him as he did. Clark undoubtedly
acted with dignity. Livingstone had had to
apologize to him and ask him to remain, and
had made the amend (to himself) by giving
him fifty dollars extra for the ten nights'
work. He could only justify the act now by
reflecting that Clark had more than once suggested investments which had turned out
most fortunately.

Livingstone determined to give Clark this
year a hundred dollars—no, fifty—he must
not spoil him, and it really was not "business."

The thought of his liberality brought to

[17]

Livingstone's mind the donations that he
always made at the close of the year. He
might as well send off the cheques now.

He took from a locked drawer his private
cheque-book and turned the stubs thought-
fully. He had had that cheque-book for a
good many years. He used to give away a
tenth of his income. His father before him
used to do that. He remembered, with a
smile, how large the sums used to seem to
him. He turned back the stubs only to see
how small a tenth used to be. He no longer
gave a tenth or a twentieth or even a—he
had no difficulty in deciding the exact per-
centage he gave; for whenever he thought
now of the sum he was worth, the figures
themselves, in clean-cut lines, popped before
his eyes. It was very curious. He could actually see them in his own handwriting. He
rubbed his eyes, and the figures disappeared.

Well, he gave a good deal, anyhow—a good

deal more than most men, he reflected. He looked at the later stubs and was gratified to find how large the amounts were, — they showed how rich he was, — and what a diversified list of charities he contributed to: hospitals, seminaries, asylums, churches, soup-kitchens, training schools of one kind or another. The stubs all bore the names of those through whom he contributed — they were mostly fashionable women of his acquaintance, who either for diversion or from real charity were interested in these institutions.

Mrs. Wright's name appeared oftenest. Mrs. Wright was a woman of fortune and very prominent, he reflected, but she was really kind; she was just a crank, and, somehow, she appeared really to believe in him. Her husband, Livingstone did not like : a cold, selfish man, who cared for nothing but money-making and his own family.

There was one name down on the book for

a small amount which Livingstone could not recall.—Oh yes, he was an assistant preacher at Livingstone's church: the donation was for a Christmas-tree in a Children's Hospital, or something of the kind. This was one of Mrs. Wright's charities too. Livingstone remembered the note the preacher had written him afterwards—it had rather jarred on him, it was so grateful. He hated "gush," he said to himself; he did not want to be bothered with details of yarn-gloves, flannel petticoats, and toys. He took out his pencil and wrote Mrs. Wright's name on the stub. That also should be charged to Mrs. Wright. He carried in his mind the total amount of the contributions, and as he came to the end a half-frown rested on his brow as he thought of having to give to all these objects again.

That was the trouble with charities,—they were as regular as coupons. Confound Mrs. Wright! Why did she not let him alone!

However, she was an important woman—the leader in the best set in the city. Livingstone sat forward and began to fill out his cheques. Certain cheques he always filled out himself. He could not bear to let even Clark know what he gave to certain objects.

The thought of how commendable this was crossed his face and lit it up like a glint of transient sunshine. It vanished suddenly as he began to calculate, leaving the place where it had rested colder than before. He really could not spend as much this year as last— why, there was—for pictures, so much; charities, so much, etc. It would quite cut into the amount he had already decided to lay by. He must draw in somewhere : he was worth only — the line of figures slipped in before his eyes with its lantern-slide coldness.

He reflected. He must cut down on his charities. He could not reduce the sum for the General Hospital Fund; he had been

[21]

SANTA CLAUS'S PARTNER

giving to that a number of years.—Nor that
for the asylum; Mrs. Wright was the presi-
dent of that board, and had told him she
counted on him.—Hang Mrs. Wright! It was
positive blackmail!—Nor the pew-rent; that
was respectable—nor the Associated Charities; every one gave to that. He must cut
out the smaller charities.

So he left off the Children's Hospital
Christmas-tree Fund, and the soup-kitchen,
and a few insignificant things like them into
which he had been worried by Mrs. Wright
and other troublesome women. The only regret he had was that taken together these
sums did not amount to a great deal. To
bring the saving up he came near cutting
out the hospital. However, he decided not to
do so. Mrs. Wright believed in him. He would
leave out one of the pictures he had intended
to buy; he would deny himself, and not cut
out the big charity. This would save him

[22]

SANTA CLAUS'S PARTNER

the trouble of refusing Mrs. Wright and would also save him a good deal more money.

Once more, at the thought of his self-denial, that ray of wintry sunshine passed across Livingstone's cold face and gave it a look of distinction—almost like that of a marble statue.

Again he relapsed into reflection. His eyes were resting on the pane outside of which the fine snow was filling the chilly afternoon air in flurries and scurries that rose and fell and seemed to be blowing every way at once. But Livingstone's eyes were not on the snow. It had been so long since Livingstone had given a thought to the weather, except as it might affect the net earnings of railways in which he was interested, that he never knew what the weather was, and so far as he was concerned there need not have been any weather. Spring was to him but the season when certain work could be done which in time would yield a crop of dividends; and

SANTA CLAUS'S PARTNER

Autumn was but the time when crops would be moved and stocks sent up or down.

So, though Livingstone's eyes rested on the pane, outside of which the flurrying snow was driving that meant so much to so many people, and his face was thoughtful—very thoughtful—he was not thinking of the snow, he was calculating profits.

CHAPTER III

A NOISE in the outer office recalled Livingstone from his reverie. He aroused himself, almost with a start, and glanced at the gilt clock just above the stock-indicator. He had been so absorbed that he had quite forgotten that he had told the clerks to wait for him. He had had no idea that he had been at work so long. He reflected, however, that he had been writing charity-cheques: the clerks ought to appreciate the fact.

He touched a button, and the next second there was a gentle tap on the door, and Clark appeared. He was just the person to give just such a tap: a refined-looking, middle-aged, middle-sized man, with a face rather pale and a little worn; a high, calm forehead, above which the grizzled hair was almost gone; mild, blue eyes which beamed through black-rimmed glasses; a pleasant mouth which a drooping, colorless moustache only partly concealed, and a well-formed but slightly retreating chin. His figure was inclined to be stout, and his shoulders were slightly bent. He walked softly, and as he spoke his voice was gentle and pleasing. There was no assertion in it, but it was perfectly self-respecting. The eyes and voice redeemed the face from being commonplace.

"Oh!—Mr. Clark, I did not know I should have been so long about my work. I was so engaged getting my book straight for you, and writing—a few cheques for my annual contributions to hospitals, etc.,—that the time slipped by—"

The tone was unusually conciliatory for Livingstone; but he still retained it in addressing Clark. It was partly a remnant of his old time relation to Mr. Clark when he, yet a young man, first knew him, and partly a recognition of Clark's position as a man of good birth who had been unfortunate, and had a large family to support.

"Oh! that's all right, Mr. Livingstone," said the clerk, pleasantly.

He gathered up the letters on the desk and was unconsciously pressing them into exact order.

"Shall I have these mailed or sent by a messenger?"

"Mail them, of course," said Livingstone. "And Clark, I want you to—"

"I thought possibly that, as to-morrow is—" began the clerk in explanation, but stopped as Livingstone continued speaking without noticing the interruption.

—"I have been going over my matters," pursued Livingstone, "and they are in excellent shape—better this year than ever before—"

The clerk's face brightened.

[27]

"That's very good," said he, heartily. "I knew they were."

—"Yes, very good, indeed," said Livingstone condescendingly, pausing to dwell for a second on the sight of the line of pallid figures which suddenly flashed before his eyes. "And I have got everything straight for you this year; and I want you to come up to my house this evening and go over the books with me quietly, so that I can show you—"

"This evening?" The clerk's countenance fell and the words were as near an exclamation as he ever indulged in.

"Yes—, this evening. I shall be at home this evening and to-morrow evening—Why not this evening?" demanded Livingstone almost sharply.

"Why, only—that it's—. However,—" The speaker broke off. "I'll be there, sir. About eight-thirty, I suppose?"

"Yes," said Livingstone, curtly.

He was miffed, offended, aggrieved. He had intended to do a kind thing by this man, and he had met with a rebuff.

" I expect to pay you," he said, coldly.

The next second he knew he had made an error. A shocked expression came involuntarily over the other's face.

"Oh! it was not that!—It was—" He paused, reflected half a second. "I'll be there," he added, and, turning quickly, withdrew, leaving Livingstone feeling very blank and then somewhat angry. He was angry with himself for making such a blunder, and then angrier with the clerk for leading him into it.

"That is the way with such people!" he reflected. "What is the use of being considerate and generous? No one appreciates it!"

The more he thought of it, the warmer he became. "Had he not taken Clark up ten— fifteen years ago, when he had not a cent in the world, and now he was getting fifteen hundred

[29]

dollars a year—yes, sixteen hundred, and almost owned his house ; and he had made every cent for him !"

At length, Livingstone's sense of injury became so strong, he could stand it no longer. He determined to have a talk with Clark.

He opened the door and walked into the outer office. One of the younger clerks was just buttoning up his overcoat. Livingstone detected a scowl on his face. The sight did not improve Livingstone's temper. He would have liked to discharge the boy on the spot. How often had he ever called on them to wait ? He knew men who required their clerks to wait always until they themselves left the office, no matter what the hour was. He himself would not do this ; he regarded it as selfish. But now when it had happened by accident, this was the return he received !

He contented himself with asking somewhat sharply where Mr. Clark was.

"Believe he's gone to the telephone," said the clerk, sulkily. He picked up his hat and said good-night hurriedly. He was evidently glad to get off.

Livingstone returned to his own room; but left the door ajar so that he could see Clark when he returned. When, however, a few moments afterwards Clark appeared Livingstone had cooled down. Why should he expect gratitude? He did not pay Clark for gratitude, but for work, and this the clerk did faithfully. It was an ungrateful world, anyhow.

At that moment there was a light knock at the outer door, and, on Clark's bidding, some one entered.

Livingstone, from where he sat, could see the door reflected in a mirror that hung in his office.

The visitor was a little girl. She was clad in a red jacket, and on her head was a red cap, from under which her hair pushed in a profusion of ringlets. Her cheeks were like apples, and her whole face was glowing from the frosty air. It was just her head that Livingstone saw first, as she poked it in and peeped around. Then, as Mr. Clark sat with his back to the door and she saw that no one else was present, the visitor inserted her whole body and, closing the door softly, with her eyes dancing and her little mouth puckered up in a mischievous way, she came on tiptoe across the floor, stealing towards Clark until she was within a few feet of him, when with a sudden little rush she threw her arms about his head and clapped her hands quickly over his eyes:

"Guess who it is?" she cried.

Livingstone could hear them through the open door.

"Blue Beard," hazarded Mr. Clark.

"No—o!"

"Queen Victoria?"

"No—o—o!"

[32]

"GUESS WHO IT IS," SHE CRIED.

"Mary, Queen of Scots?—I know it's a queen."

"No. Now you are not guessing— It is n't any queen, at all."

"Yes, I am—Oh! I know—Santa Claus."

"No; but somebody 'at knows about him."

"Mr. L—m—m—"

Livingstone was not sure that he caught the name.

"No!!" in a very emphatic voice and with a sudden stiffening and a vehement shake of the head.

Livingstone knew now whose name it was.

"Now, if you guess right this time, you'll get a reward."

"What reward?"

"Why,—Santa Claus will bring you a whole lot of nice—"

"I don't believe that;—he will be too busy with some other folks I know, who—"

"No, he won't—I know he's going to bring

[33]

you — Oh!" She suddenly took one hand from Clark's eyes and clapped it over her mouth — but next second replaced it.—"And besides, I'll give you a whole lot of kisses."

"Oh! yes, I know—the Princess with the Golden Locks, Santa Claus's Partner — the sweetest little kitten in the world, and her name is—Kitty Clark."

"Umhm——m!" And on a sudden, the arms were transferred from about the forehead to the neck and the little girl, with her sunny head canted to one side, was making good her promise of reward. Livingstone could hear the kisses.

The next second they moved out of the line of reflection in Livingstone's mirror. But he could still catch fragments of what they said. Clark spoke too low to be heard; but now and then, Livingstone could catch the little girl's words. Indeed, he could not help hearing her.

"Oh! papa!" she exclaimed in a tone of

[34]

disappointment, replying to something her father had told her.

"But papa you *must* come — You *promised!*"

Again her father talked to her low and soothingly.

"But papa — I 'm so disappointed — I 've saved all my money just to have you go with me. And mamma — I 'll go and ask him to let you come."

Her father evidently did not approve of this, and the next moment he led the child to the door, still talking to her soothingly, and Livingstone heard him kiss her and tell her to wait for him below.

Livingstone let himself out of his side-door. He did not want to meet Clark just then. He was not in a comfortable frame of mind. He had a little headache.

As he turned into the street, he passed the little girl he had seen up-stairs. She was wiping her little, smeared face with her handkerchief, and had evidently been crying. Livingstone, as he passed, caught her eye, and she gave him such a look of hate that it stung him to the quick.

"The little serpent!" thought he. " Here he was supporting her family, and she looking as if she could tear him to pieces! It showed how ungrateful this sort of people were."

CHAPTER IV

LIVINGSTONE walked up town. It would, he felt, do his head good. He needed exercise. He had been working rather too hard of late. However, he was worth—yes, all that!—Out in the snow the sum was before him in cold facsimile.

He had not gone far before he wished he had ridden. The street was thronged with people: some streaming along; others stopping in front of the big shop-windows, blocking the way and forcing such as were in a hurry to get off the sidewalk. The shop-windows were all brilliantly dressed and lighted. Every conception of fertile brains was there to arrest the attention and delight the imagination. And the interest of the throngs outside and in testified the shopkeepers' success.

Here Santa Claus, the last survivor of the

old benefactors, who has outlasted whole hie-
rarchies of outworn myths and, yet firm in the
devotion of the heart of childhood, snaps his
fingers alike at arid science and blighting
stupidity, was driving his reindeer, his teem-
ing sleigh filled with wonders from every
region : dolls that walked and talked and
sang, fit for princesses; sleds fine enough for
princes; drums and trumpets and swords for
young heroes; horses that looked as though
they were alive and would spring next moment from their rockers; bats and balls that
almost started of themselves from their places;
little uniforms, and frocks; skates; tennis-
racquets; baby caps and rattles; tiny engines
and coaches; railway trains; animals that ran
about; steamships; books; pictures — everything to delight the soul of childhood and
gratify the affection of age.

There Kris Kringle, Santa Claus's other self,
with snowy beard, and fur coat hoary with the

frost of Arctic travel from the land of unfailing snow and unfailing toys, stood beside his
tree glittering with crystal and shining with
the fruits of every industry and every clime.

These were but a part of the dazzling display that was ever repeated over and over
and filled the windows for squares and squares.
Science and Art appeared to have combined
to pay tribute to childhood. The very street
seemed to have blossomed with Christmas.

But Livingstone saw nothing of it. He
was filled with anger that his way should be
blocked. The crowds were gay and cheery.
Strangers in sheer good-will clapped each
other on the shoulder and exchanged views,
confidences and good wishes. The truck-driv-
ers, usually so surly, drew out of each others'
way and shouted words of cheer after their
smiling fellows.

The soul of Christmas was abroad on the air.

Livingstone did not even recall what day it

[39]

was. All he saw was a crowd of fools that impeded his progress. He tried the middle of the street; but the carriages and delivery-wagons were so thick, that he turned off, growling, and took a less frequented thoroughfare, a back street of mean houses and small shops where a poorer class of people dwelt and dealt.

Here, however, he was perhaps even more incommoded than he had been before. This street was, if anything, more crowded than the other and with a more noisy and hilarious throng. Here, instead of fine shops, there were small ones; but their windows were every bit as attractive to the crowds on the street as those Livingstone had left. People of a much poorer class surged in and out of the doors; small gamins, some in ragged overcoats, more in none, gabbled with and shouldered each other boisterously at the windows and pressed their red noses to the frosty panes, to see through the blurred patches made by their warm breath the wondrous marvels within. The little pastry-shops and corner-groceries vied with the toy-shops and confectionaries, and were packed with a population that hummed like bees, the busy murmur broken every now and then by jests and calls and laughter, as the customers squeezed in empty-handed, or slipped out with carefully-wrapped parcels hugged close to their cheery bosoms or carried in their arms with careful pride.

Livingstone finally was compelled to get off the sidewalk again and take to the street. Here, at least, there were no fine carriages to block his way.

As he began to approach a hill, he was aware of yells of warning ahead of him, and, with shouts of merriment, a swarm of sleds began to shoot by him, some with dark objects lying flat on their little stomachs, kicking their heels high in the air; others with small

[41]

single or double or triple headed monsters seated upright and all screaming at the top of their merry voices. All were unmindful of the falling snow and nipping air, their blood hot with the ineffable fire of youth that flames in the warm heart of childhood, glows in that of youth, and cools only with the cooling brain and chilling pulse.

Before Livingstone could press back into the almost solid mass on the sidewalk he had come near being run down a score of times. He felt that it was an outrage. He fairly flamed with indignation. He, a large tax-payer, a generous contributor to asylums and police funds, a supporter of hospitals,—that he should be almost killed!

He looked around for a policeman—

"Whoop! Look out! Get out the way!" Swish! Swish! Swish! they shot by. Livingstone had to dodge for his life. Of course, no policeman was in sight!

LIVINGSTONE HAD TO DODGE FOR HIS LIFE.

Livingstone pushed his way on to the top
of the ascent, and a square further on he
found an officer inspecting silently a group of
noisy urchins squabbling over the division of
two sticks of painted candy. His back was
towards the hill from which were coming the
shouts of the sliding miscreants.

Livingstone accosted him:

"That sliding, back there, must be stopped.
It is a nuisance," he asserted.—It was dan-
gerous, he declared; he himself had almost
been struck by one or more of those sleds and
if it had run him down it might have killed
him.

The officer, after a long look at him, turned
silently and walked slowly in the direction of
the hill. He moved so deliberately and with
such evident reluctance that Livingstone's
blood boiled. He hurried after him.

" Here," he said, as he overtook him, "I
am going to see that you stop that sliding and

[43]

enforce the law, or I shall report you for failure to perform your duty. I see your number —268."

"All right, sir. You can do as you please about that," said the officer, rather surlily, but politely.

Livingstone walked close after him to the hilltop. The officer spoke a few words in a quiet tone to the boys who were at the summit, and instantly every sled stopped. Not so the tongues. Babel broke loose. Some went off in silence; others crowded about the officer, expostulating, cajoling, grumbling. It was "the first snow;" they "always slid on that hill;" "it did not hurt anybody;" "nobody cared," etc.

"This gentleman has complained, and you must stop," said the officer.

They all turned on Livingstone with sudden hate.

"Arr-oh-h!" they snarled in concert. "We

aint a-hurtin' him! What's he got to do wid us anyhow!"

One more apt archer than the rest, shouted, "He ain't no gentleman—a *gentleman* don't never interfere wid poor little boys what ain't a-done him no harm!"

But they stopped, and the more timid or impatient stole off to find new and less inconveniently guarded inclines.

Livingstone passed on. He did not know that the moment he left and the officer turned his back, the whole hillside swarmed again into life and fun and joy. He did not know this; but he bore off with him a new thorn which even his feeling of civic virtue could not keep from rankling. His head ached, and he grew crosser and crosser with every step.

He had never seen so many beggars. It was insufferable. For this evening, at least, every one was giving—except Livingstone. Want was stretching out its withered hand even

[45]

to Poverty and found it filled. But Livingstone took no part in it. The chilly and threadbare street-venders of shoe-strings, pencils and cheap flowers, who to-night were offering in their place tin toys, mistletoe and holly-boughs, he pushed roughly out of his way; he snapped angrily at beggars who had the temerity to accost him.

"Confound them! They ought to be run in by the police!"

A red-faced, collarless man fell into the same gait with him, and in a cajoling tone began to mutter something of his distress.

"Be off. Go to the Associated Charities," snarled Livingstone, conscious of the biting sarcasm of his speech.

"Go where, sir?"

"Go to the devil!"

The man stopped in his tracks.

A ragged, meagre boy slid in through the crowd just ahead of Livingstone, to a woman who was toiling along with a large bundle. Holding out a pinched hand, he offered to carry the parcel for her. The woman hesitated.

—"For five cents," he pleaded.

. She was about to yield, for the bundle was heavy. But the boy was just in front of Livingstone and in his eagerness brushed against him. Livingstone gave him a shove which sent him spinning away across the sidewalk; the stream of passers-by swept in between them, and the boy lost his job and the woman his service.

The man of success passed on.

CHAPTER V

I F Livingstone had been in a huff when he left his office, by the time he reached his home he was in a rage.

As he let himself in with his latch-key his expression for a moment softened. The scene before him was one which might well have mellowed a man just out of the snowy street. A spacious and handsome house, both richly and artistically furnished, lay before him. Rich furniture, costly rugs, fine pictures and rare books, gave evidence not only of his wealth but of his taste. He was not a mere business machine, a mere money-maker. He knew men who were. He despised them. He was a man of taste and culture, a gentleman of refinement. He spent his money like a gentleman, to surround himself with objects of art and to give himself and his friends pleasure. Connoisseurs came to look at his fine collection and to revel in his rare editions. Dealers had told him his collection was worth double what it had cost him. He had frowned at the suggestion; but it was satisfactory to know it.

As Livingstone entered his library and found a bright fire burning; his favorite armchair drawn up to his especial table; his favorite books lying within easy reach, he felt a momentary glow.

He stretched himself out before the fire in his deep lounging-chair with a feeling of relief. The next moment, however, he was sensible of his fatigue, and was conscious that he had quite a headache. What a fool he had been to walk up through the snow! And those people had worried him!

His head throbbed. He had been working too hard of late. He would go and see his doctor next day and talk it over with him. He could now take his advice and stop working for a while; he was worth—Confound those figures! Why could not he think of them without their popping in before his eyes that way!

There was a footfall on the heavily carpeted floor behind him, so soft that it could scarcely be said to have made a sound, but Livingstone caught it. He spoke without turning his head.

"James!"

"Yes, sir. Have you dined, sir?"

"Dined? No, of course not! Where was I to dine?"

"I thought perhaps you had dined at the club. I will have dinner directly, sir," said the butler quietly.

"Dine at the club! Why should I dine at the club? Haven't I my own house to dine in?" demanded Livingstone.

"Yes, sir. We had dinner ready, only—as you were so late we thought perhaps you were dining at the club. You had not said anything about dining out."

[50]

Livingstone glanced at the clock. It was half-past eight. He had had no idea it was so late. He had forgotten how late it was when he left his office, and the walk through the snow had been slow. He was hopelessly in the wrong.

Just then there was a scurry in the hall outside and the squeak of childish voices. James coughed and turned quickly towards the door.

Livingstone wanted an outlet.

"What is that?" he asked, sharply.

James cleared his throat nervously. The squeak came again — this time almost a squeal.

"Whose children are those?" demanded Livingstone.

"Ahem! I thinks they's the laundress's, sir. They just came around this evening — "

Livingstone cut him short.

"Well! I — !" He was never nearer an outbreak, but he controlled himself.

"Go down and send them and her off immediately; and you—" He paused, closed his lips firmly, and changed his speech. "I wish some dinner," he said coldly.

"Yes, sir."

James had reached the door when he turned.

"Shall you be dining at home to-morrow, sir?" he asked, quietly.

"Yes, of course," said Livingstone, shortly. "And I don't want to see any one to-night, no matter who comes. I am tired." He had forgotten Clark.

"Yes, sir."

The butler withdrew noiselessly, and Livingstone sank back in his chair. But before the butler was out of hearing Livingstone recalled him.

"I don't want any dinner."

"Can have it for you directly, sir," said James, persuasively.

"I say I don't want any."

James came a little closer and gave his master a quick glance.

"Are you feeling bad, sir?" he asked.

"No, I only want to be let alone. I shall go out presently to the club."

This time James withdrew entirely.

What happened when James passed through the door which separated his domain from his master's was not precisely what Livingstone had commanded. What the tall butler did was to gather up in his arms two very plump little tots who at sight of him came running to him with squeals of joy, flinging themselves on him, and choking him with their chubby arms, to the imminent imperiling of his immaculate linen.

Taking them both up together, James bore them off quietly to some remote region where he filled their little mouths full of delightful candy which kept their little jaws working

[53]

tremendously and their blue eyes opening and shutting in unison, whilst he told them of the dreadful unnamed things that would befall them if they ventured again through that door. He impressed on them the calamity it would be to lose the privilege of holding the evergreens whilst they were being put up in the hall, and the danger of Santa Claus passing by that night without filling their stockings.

The picture he drew of two little stockings hanging limp and empty at the fireplace while Santa Claus went by with bulging sleigh was harrowing.

At mention of it, the tots both looked down at their stockings and were so over-come that they almost stopped working their jaws, so that when they began again they were harder to work than ever. To this James added the terror of their failing to see next day the great plum-pudding suddenly burst into flame in his hands. At this, he threw up both hands and opened them so wide that the little ones had to look first at one of his hands and then at the other to make sure that he was not actually holding the dancing flames now.

When they had promised faithfully and with deep awe, crossing their little hearts with smudgy fingers, the butler entrusted them to some one to see to the due performance of their good intention, and he himself sought the cook, who, next to himself, was Livingstone's oldest servant. She was at the moment, with plump arms akimbo on her stout waist, laying down the law of marriage to a group of merry servants as they sorted Christmas wreaths.

"Wait till you've known a man twenty years before you marry him, and then you'll never marry him," she said. The point of her advice being that she was past forty and had never married.

The butler beckoned her out and confided to her his anxiety.

"He is not well," he said gloomily. "I have not see him this a-way in ten years. He is not well."

The cook's cheery countenance changed.

"But you say he have had no dinner." Her excessive grammar was a reassurance. She turned alertly towards her range.

"But he won't have dinner."

"What!" The stiffness went out of her form in visible detachments. "Then he air sick!"

She made one attempt to help matters. "Can't I make him something nice? Very nice?—And light?" She brightened at the hope.

"No, nothink. He will not hear to it."

"Then you must have the doctor." She spoke decisively.

To this the butler made no reply, at least in words. He stood wrapt in deep abstraction, his face filled with perplexity and gloom, and as the cook watched him anxiously her face too took on gradually the same expression.

"I has not see him like this before, not in ten year—not in twelve year. Not since he got that letter from that young lady what—." He stopped and looked at the cook.—"He was hactually hirascible!"

"He must be got to bed, poor dear!" said the cook, sympathetically. "And you must get the doctor, and I'll make some good rich broth to have it handy.—And just when we were a-goin' to dress the house and have it so beautiful!"

She turned away, her round face full of woe.

"Ah! Well!—" The butler tried to find some sentence that might be comforting; but before he could secure one that suited, the door bell rang, and he went to answer it.

CHAPTER VI

IT was Mr. Clark, who as soon as the door was opened stepped within and taking off his hat began to shake the snow from it, even while he greeted James and wished him a merry Christmas.

James liked Mr. Clark. He did not rate him very highly in the matter of intelligence; but he recognized him as a gentleman, and appreciated his kindly courtesy to himself. He knew it came from a good heart.

Many a man who drove up to the door in a carriage, James relieved of his coat and showed into the drawing-room in silence; but the downcast eyes were averted to conceal inconvenient thoughts and the expressionless face was a mask to hide views which the caller might not have cared to discover. Mr. Clark, however, always treated James with consideration, and James re-

[58]

ciprocated the feeling and returned the treatment.

Mr. Clark was giving James his hat when the butler took in that he had come to see Mr. Livingstone.

"Mr. Livingstone begs to be excused this evening, sir," he said.

"Yes." Mr. Clark laid a package on a chair and proceeded to unbutton his overcoat.

"He says he regrets he cannot see any one," explained the servant.

"Yes. That's all right. I know." He caught the lapels of the coat preparatory to taking it off.

"No, sir. He cannot see *anybody* at all this evening," insisted James, confident in being within his authority.

"Why, he told me to come and bring his books! I suppose he meant—!"

"No, sir. He is not very well this evening."

Mr. Clark's hands dropped to his side.

"Not well! Why, he left the office only an hour or two ago."

"Yes, sir; but he walked up, and seemed very tired when he arrived. He did not eat anything, and—the doctor is coming to see him."

Mr. Clark's face expressed the deepest concern.

"He has been working too hard," he said, shaking his head. " He ought to have let me go over those accounts. With all he has to carry!"

"Yes, sir, that's it," said James, heartily.

"Well, don't you think I'd better go up and see him?" asked the old clerk, solicitously. "I might be able to suggest something?"

"No, sir. He said quite positive he would not see *anybody*." James looked the clerk full in the face. "I was afraid something might 'ave 'appened down in the—ah—?"

Mr. Clark's face lit up with a kindly light.

"No, indeed. It's nothing like that, James. We never had so good a year. You can make your mind easy about that."

"Thank you, sir," said the servant. "We'll have the doctor drop in to see him, and I hope he'll be all right in the morning. Snowy night, sir."

"I hope so," said Mr. Clark, not intending to convey his views as to the weather. "You'll let me know if I am wanted—if I can do anything. I will come around first thing in the morning to see how he is. I hope he'll be all right. Good-night. A merry Christmas to you."

"Good-night, sir. Thankee, sir; the same to you, sir. I'm going to wait up to see how he is. Good-night, sir."

And James shut the door softly behind the visitor, feeling a sense of comfort not wholly accounted for by the information as to the successful year. Mr. Clark, somehow, always reassured him. The butler could understand the springs that moved that kindly spirit.

What Mr. Clark thought as he tramped back through the snow need not be fully detailed. But at least, one thing was certain, he never thought of himself.

If he recalled that a mortgage would be due on his house just one week from that day, and that the doctors' bills had been unusually heavy that year, it was not on his own account that he was anxious. Indeed, he never considered himself; there were too many others to think of. One thought was that he was glad his friend had such a good servant as James to look after him. Another was pity that Livingstone had never known the joy that was awaiting himself when at the end of that mile of snow he should peep into the little cosy back room (for the front room was mysteriously closed this evening), where a sweet-faced, frail-looking woman would be lying on a lounge with a half-dozen little curly heads bobbing about her. He knew what a scream of delight would greet him as he poked his head in; and out in the darkness and cold John Clark smiled and smacked his lips as he thought of the kisses and squeezes, and renewed kisses that would be his lot as he told how he would be with them all the evening.

Yes, he was undoubtedly sorry for Livingstone, a poor lonely man in that great house; and he determined that he would not say much about his being ill. Women did not always exactly understand some men, and when he left home, Mrs. Clark had expressed some very strong views as to Livingstone which had pained Clark. She had even spoken of him as selfish and miserly. He would just say now that Livingstone on his arrival had sent him straight back home.

SANTA CLAUS'S PARTNER

No, Mr. Clark never thought of himself, and this made him richer than Mr. Livingstone.

When Mr. Clark reached home his expectation was more than realized. From the way in which he noiselessly opened the front door and then stole along the little passage to the back room, from which the sound of many voices was coming as though it were a mimic Babel, you might have thought he was a thief.

And when he opened the door softly and, with dancing eyes, poked his head into the room, you might have thought he was Santa Claus himself. There was one second of dead silence as a half-dozen pair of eyes stretched wide and a half-dozen mouths opened with a gasp, and then, with a shout which would have put to the blush a tribe of wild Indians, a half-dozen young bodies flung themselves upon him with screams and shrieks of delight. John Clark's neck must have been of

[64]

iron to withstand such hugs and tugs as it was given.

The next instant he was drawn bodily into the room and pushed down forcibly into a chair, whilst the whole half-dozen piled upon him with demands to be told how he had managed to get off and come back. No one but Clark could have understood them or answered them, but somehow, as his arms seemed able to gather in the whole lot of struggling, squeezing, wriggling, shoving little bodies, so his ears seemed to catch all the questions and his mind to answer each in turn and all together.

"'How did I come?'—Ran every step of the way.—'Why did I come back?'—Well! that's a question for a man with eight children who will sit up and keep Santa Claus out of the house unless their father comes home and puts them to bed and holds their eyelids down to keep them from peeping and scaring Santa Claus away!

[65]

—"'What did Mr. Livingstone say?'— Well, what do you suppose a man would say Christmas Eve to another man who has eight wide-awake children who will sit up in front of the biggest fire-place in the house until midnight Christmas Eve so that Santa Claus can't come down the only chimney big enough to hold his presents? He would say, 'John Clark, I have no children of my own, but you have eight, and if you don't go home this minute and see that those children are in bed and fast asleep and snoring,— yes, snoring, mind,—by ten o'clock, I'll never, and Santa Claus will never—!'

—"'Did I see anything of Santa Claus?' Well, if I were to tell you—what I saw this night, why, — you'd never believe me. There's a sleigh so big coming in a little while to this town, and this street, and this house, that it holds presents enough for—.

"'When will it be here?' Well, from the

[66]

SANTA CLAUS'S PARTNER

sleigh-bells that I heard I should say—. My
goodness, gracious! If it is n't almost ten
o'clock, and if that sleigh should get here
whilst there 's a single eye open in this
house, I don't know what Santa Claus might
do!"

And, with a strength that one might have
thought quite astonishing, John Clark rose
somehow from under the mass of little heads,
and, with his arms still around them, still talking, still cajoling, still entertaining and still
caressing, he managed to bear the whole
curly, chattering flock to the door where,
with renewed kisses and squeezes and questions, they were all finally induced to release
their hold and run squeaking and frisking off
upstairs to bed.

Then, as he closed the door, Clark turned
and looked at the only other occupant of the
room, a lady whose pale face would have
told her story even had she not remained

[67]

outstretched on a lounge during the preceding scene.

If, however, Mrs. Clark's face was pale, her eyes were brilliant, and the look that she and her husband exchanged told that even invalidism and narrow means have alleviations, so full was the glance they gave of confidence and joy.

Yet, as absolute as was their confidence, Mr. Clark did not now tell his wife the truth. He gave her in a few words the reason of his return. Mr. Livingstone was feeling unwell, he said. He had not remembered it was Christmas Eve, he added; and, turning quickly and opening the door into the front room he guilefully dived at once into the matter of the Christmas-tree which was standing there waiting to be dressed.

Whether or not Mr. Clark deceived Mrs. Clark might be a matter of question. Mr. Clark was not good at deception. Mrs. Clark

was better at it; but then, to-night was a
night of peace and good-will, and since her
husband had returned she was willing to forgive even Livingstone.

CHAPTER VII

LIVINGSTONE, at this moment, was not feeling as wealthy as the row of figures in clean-cut lines that were now beginning to be almost constantly before his eyes might have seemed to warrant. He was sitting sunk deep in his cushioned arm-chair. The tweaks in his forehead that had annoyed him earlier in the evening had changed to twinges, and the twinges had now given place to a dull, steady ache. And every thought of his wealth brought that picture of seven staring figures before his eyes, whilst, in place of the glow which they had brought at first, he now at every recollection of them had a cold thrill of apprehension lest they might appear.

James's inquiry, "Shall you be dining at home to-morrow?" had recurred to him and now disturbed him. It was a simple question; nothing remarkable in it. It now came to him that to-morrow was Christmas Day, and he had forgotten it. This was remarkable. He had never forgotten it before, but this year he had been working so hard and had been so engrossed he had not thought of it. Even this reflection brought the spectral figures back sharply outlined before his eyes. They stayed longer now. He must think of something else.

He thought of Christmas. This was the first Christmas he had ever been at home by himself. A Christmas dinner alone! Who had ever heard of such a thing! He must go out to dinner, of course. He glanced over at his table where James always put his mail. Everything was in perfect order: the book he had read the night before; the evening paper and the last financial quotation were all there; but not a letter. James must have forgot them.

He turned to rise and ring the bell and

glanced across the room towards it. What a dark room it was! What miserable gas!

He turned up the light at his hand. It did not help perceptibly. He sank back. What selfish dogs people were, he reflected. Of all the hosts of people he knew, people who had entertained him and whom he had entertained,—not one had thought to invite him to the Christmas dinner. A dozen families at whose houses he had often been entertained flashed across his mind. Why, years ago he used to have a half-dozen invitations to Christmas dinner, and now he had not one! Even Mrs. Wright, to whom he had just sent a contribution for—Hello! that lantern-slide again! It would not do to think of figures. — Even she had not thought of him.

There must be some reason? he pondered. Yes, Christmas dinners were always family reunions—that was the reason he was left out and forgotten;—yes, forgotten. A list of the people who he knew would have such reunions came to him;—almost every one of his acquaintances had a family;—even Clark had a family and would have a Christmas dinner.

At the thought, a pang almost of envy of Clark smote him.

Suddenly his own house seemed to grow vast and empty and lonely; he felt perfectly desolate,—abandoned—alone—ill! He glanced around at his pictures. They were cold, staring, stony, dead! The reflection of the cross lights made them look ghastly.

As he gazed at them the figures they had cost shot before his eyes. My God! he could not stand this! He sprang to his feet. Even the pain of getting up was a relief. He stared around him. Dead silence and stony faces were all about him. The capacious room seemed a vast, empty cavern, and as he stood he saw stretching before him his whole future life

SANTA CLAUS'S PARTNER

spent in this house, as lonely, silent, and desolate as this. It was unbearable.

He walked through to his drawing-room.
The furniture was sheeted, the room colder
and lonelier a thousand-fold than the other;
—on into the dining-room;—the bare table
in the dim light looked like ice; the sideboard
with its silver and glass, bore sheets of ice.
"Pshaw!" He turned up the lights. He would
take a drink of brandy and go to bed.

He took a decanter, poured out a drink and
drained it off. His hand trembled, but the
stimulant helped him a little. It enabled him
to collect his ideas and think. But his
thoughts still ran on Christmas and his loneliness.

Why should not he give a Christmas dinner
and invite his friends? Yes, that was what he
would do. Whom should he ask? His mind
began to run over the list. Every one he
knew had his own house; and as to friends

—why, he didn't have any friends! He had
only acquaintances. He stopped suddenly, ap-
palled by the fact. He had not a friend in the
world! Why was it? In answer to the thought
the seven figures flashed into sight. He put
his hand to his eyes to shut them out. He
knew now why. He had been too busy to
make friends. He had given his youth and his
middle manhood to accumulate—those seven
figures again!—And he had given up his
friendships. He was now almost aged.

He walked into his drawing-room and
turned up the light—all the lights to look
at himself in a big mirror. He did look at
himself and he was confounded. He was not
only no longer young—he was prepared for
this—but he was old. He would not have
dreamed he could be so old. He was gray
and wrinkled.

As he faced himself his blood seemed suddenly to chill. He was conscious of a sensible

ebb as if the tide about his heart had suddenly sunk lower. Perhaps, it was the cooling
of the atmosphere as the fire in his library
died out, — or was it his blood?

He went back into his library not ten minutes, but ten years older than when he left it.

He sank into his chair and insensibly began
to scan his life. He had just seen himself as
he was; he now saw himself as he had been
long ago, and saw how he had become what
he was. The whole past lay before him like a
slanting pathway.

He followed it back to where it began — in
an old home far off in the country.

He was a very little boy. All about was the
bustle and stir of preparation for Christmas.
Cheer was in every face, for it was in every
heart. Boxes were coming from the city by
every conveyance. The store-room and closets
were centres of unspeakable interest, shrouded
in delightful mystery. The kitchen was lighted

by the roaring fire and steaming from the numberless good things preparing for the next day's feast. Friends were arriving from the distant railway and were greeted with universal delight. The very rigor of the weather was deemed a part of the Christmas joy, for it was known that Santa Claus with his jingling sleigh came the better through the deeper snow. Everything gave the little boy joy, particularly going with his father and mother to bear good things to poor people who lived in smaller houses. They were always giving; but Christmas was the season for a more general and generous distribution. He recalled across forty years his father and mother putting the presents into his hands to bestow, and his father's words, "My boy, learn the pleasure of giving."

The rest was all blaze and light and glow, and his father and mother moving about like shining spirits amid it all.

SANTA CLAUS'S PARTNER

Then he was a schoolboy, measuring the
lagging time by the coming Christmas; count-
ing the weeks, the days, the hours in an ecs-
tasy of impatience until he should be free
from the drudgery of books and the slavery
of classes, and should be able to start for home
with the friends who had leave to go with
him. How slowly the time crept by, and how
he told the other boys of the joys that would
await them! And when it had really gone,
and they were free! how delicious it used to
be!

As the scene appeared before him Livingstone could almost feel again the thrill that
set him quivering with delight; the boundless
joy that filled his veins as with an elixir.

The arrival at the station drifted before him
and the pride of his introduction of the servants whose faces shone with pleasure; the
drive home through the snow, which used
somehow to be warming, not chilling, in those

days; and then, through the growing dusk, the first sight of the home-light, set, he knew, by the mother in her window as a beacon shining from the home and mother's heart. Then the last, toilsome climb up the home-hill and the outpouring of welcome amid cheers and shouts and laughter.

Oh, the joy of that time! And through all the festivity was felt, like a sort of pervading warmth, the fact that that day Christ came into the world and brought peace and good will and cheer to every one.

The boy Livingstone saw was now installed regularly as the bearer of Christmas presents and good things to the poor, and the pleasure he took then in his office flashed across Livingstone's mind like a sudden light. It lit up the faces of many whom Livingstone had not thought of for years. They were all beaming on him now with a kindliness to which he had long been a stranger; that kindliness which belongs only to our memory of our youth.

Was it possible that he could ever have had so many friends! The man in the chair put his hand to his eyes to try and hold the beautiful vision, but it faded away, shut out from view by another.

CHAPTER VIII

THE vision that came next was of a college student. The Christmas holidays were come again. They were still as much the event of the year as when he was a schoolboy. Once more he was on his way home accompanied by friends whom he had brought to help him enjoy the holidays, his enjoyment doubled by their enjoyment. Once more, as he touched the soil of his own neighborhood, from a companion he became a host. Once more with his friends he reached his old home and was received with that greeting which he never met with elsewhere. He saw his father and mother standing on the wide portico before the others with outstretched arms, affection and pride beaming in their faces. He witnessed their cordial greeting of his friends. "Our son's friends are our friends," he heard them say.

Henry Trelane said afterwards, " Why, Livingstone, you have told me of your home and your horses, but never told me of your father and mother. Do you know that they are the best in the world?" Somehow, it had seemed to open his eyes, and the manner in which his friends had hung on his father's words had increased his own respect for him. One of them had said, " Livingstone, I like you, but I love your father." The phrase, he remembered, had not altogether pleased him, and yet it had not altogether displeased him either. But Henry Trelane was very near to him in those days. Not only was he the soul of honor and high-mindedness, with a mind that reflected truth as an unruffled lake reflects the sky, but he was the brother of Catherine Trelane, who then stood to Livingstone for Truth itself.

It was during a Christmas-holiday visit to her brother that Livingstone had first met

Catherine Trelane; as he now saw himself meet her. He had come on her suddenly in a long avenue. Her arms were full of holly-boughs; her face was rosy from a victorious tramp through the snow, rosier at the hoped-for, unexpected, chance meeting with her brother's guest; a sprig of mistletoe was stuck daringly in her hood, guarded by her mischievous, laughing eyes. She looked like a dryad fresh from the winter woods. For years after that Livingstone had never thought of Christmas without being conscious of a certain radiance that vision shed upon the time.

The next day in the holly-dressed church she seemed a saint wrapt in divine adoration.

Another shift of the scene; another Christmas.

Reverses had come. His father, through kindness and generosity, had become involved beyond his means, and, rather than endure the least shadow of reproach, gave up everything

he possessed to save his name and shield a
friend. Livingstone himself had been called
away from college.

He remembered the sensation of it all. He
recalled the picture of his father as he stood
calm and unmoved amid the wreck of his fortune and faced unflinchingly the hard, dark
future. It was an inspiring picture : the picture of a gentleman, far past the age when
men can start afresh and achieve success,
despoiled by another and stripped of all he
had in the world, yet standing upright and
tranquil; a just man walking in his integrity;
a brave man facing the world; firm as an im-
movable rock; serene as an unblemished
morning.

Livingstone had never taken in before
how fine it was. He had at one time even
felt aggrieved by his father's act; now he was
suddenly conscious of a thrill of pride in him.

If he were only living! He himself was now

worth—! Suddenly that lantern-slide shot before his eyes and shut out the noble figure
standing there.

Livingstone's mind reverted to his own
career.

He was a young man in business; living in
a cupboard; his salary a bare pittance; yet
he was rich; he had hope and youth; family
and friends. Heavens! how rich he was then!
It made the man in the chair poor now to
feel how rich he had been then and had
not known it. He looked back at himself
with a kind of envy, strange to him, which
gave him a pain.

He saw himself again at Christmas. He
was back at the little home which his father
had taken when he lost the old place. He
saw himself unpacking his old trunk, taking
out from it the little things he had brought
as presents, with more pride than he had
ever felt before, for he had earned them him-

self. Each one represented sacrifice, thought, affection. He could see again his father's face lit up with pride and his mother's radiant with delight in his achievement. His mother was handing him her little presents, —the gloves she had knit for him herself with so much joy; the shaving-case she had herself embroidered; the cup and saucer from the old tea-service that had belonged to his great-grandfather and great-grandmother and which had been given his mother and father when they were married. He glanced up as she laid the delicate piece of Sèvres before him, and caught her smile—That smile! Was there ever another like it? It held in it—everything.

Suddenly Livingstone felt something moving on his cheek. He put his hand up to his face and when he took it down his fingers were wet.

With his mother's face, another face came to him, radiant with the beauty of youth.

Catherine Trelane, since that meeting in the long avenue, had grown more and more to him, until all other motives and aims had been merged in one radiant hope.

With his love he had grown timid; he scarcely dared look into her eyes; yet now he braved the world for her; bore for her all the privations and hardships of life in its first struggle. Indeed, for her, privation was no hardship. He was poor in purse, but rich in hope. Love lit up his life and touched the dull routine of his work with the light of enchantment. If she made him timid before her, she made him bold towards the rest of the world. 'T was for her that he had had the courage to take that plunge into the boiling sea of life in an unknown city, and it was for her that he had had strength to keep above water, where so many had gone down.

He had faced all for her and had conquered all for her. He recalled the long struggle, the painful, patient waiting, the stern self-denial. He had deliberately chosen between pleasure and success, —between the present and the future. He had denied himself to achieve his fortune, and he had succeeded.

At first, it had been for her; then Success had become dear to him for itself, had ever grown larger and dearer as he advanced, until now— A thrill of pride ran through him, which changed into a shiver as it brought those accursed, staring, ghastly figures straight before his eyes.

He had great trouble to drive the figures away. It was only when he thought fixedly of Catherine Trelane as she used to be that they disappeared. She was a vision then to banish all else. He had a picture of her somewhere among his papers. He had not seen it for years, but no picture could do her justice: as rich as was her coloring, as beautiful as were her eyes, her mouth, her *riante* face, her slim, willowy, girlish figure and fine carriage, it was not these that came to him when he thought of her; it was rather the spirit of which these were but the golden shell : it was the smile, the music, the sunshine, the radiance which came to him and warmed his blood and set his pulses throbbing across all those years. He would get the picture and look at it.

But memory swept him on.

He had got in the tide of success and the current had borne him away. First it had been the necessity to succeed ; then ambition ; then opportunity to do better and better always taking firmer hold of him and bearing him further and further until the pressure of business, change of ambition and, at last, of ideals swept him beyond sight of all he had known or cared for.

He could almost see the process of the metamorphosis. Year after year he had waited and worked and Catherine Trelane had waited ;

then had come a time when he did not wish her to wait longer. His ideals had changed. Success had come to mean but one thing for him : gold ; he no longer strove for honors but for riches. He abandoned the thought of glory and of power, of which he had once dreamed. Now he wanted gold. Beauty would fade, culture prove futile; but gold was king, and all he saw bowed before it. Why marry a poor girl when another had wealth?

He found a girl as handsome as Catherine Trelane. It was not a chapter in his history in which he took much pride. Just when he thought he had succeeded, her father had interposed and she had yielded easily. She had married a fool with ten times Livingstone's wealth. It was a blow to Livingstone, but he had recovered, and after that he had a new incentive in life ; he would be richer than her father or her husband.

He had become so and had bought his house

partly to testify to the fact. Then he had gone back to Catherine Trelane. She had come unexpectedly into property. He had not dared quite to face her, but had written to her, asking her to marry him. He had her reply somewhere now; it had cut deeper than she ever knew or would know. She wrote that the time had been when she might have married him even had he asked her by letter, but it was too late now. The man she might have loved was dead. He had gone to see her then, but had found what she said was true. She was more beautiful than when he had last seen her—so beautiful that the charm of her maturity had almost eclipsed in his mind the memory of her girlish loveliness. But she was inexorable. He had not blamed her, he had only cursed himself, and had plunged once more into the boiling current of the struggle for wealth. And he had won—yes, won!

With a shock those figures slipped before

his eyes and would not go away. Even when he shut his eyes and rubbed them the ghastly line was there.

He turned and gazed down the long room. It was as empty as a desert. He listened to see if he could hear any sound, even hoping to hear some sound from his servants. All was as silent as a tomb.

He rubbed his eyes, with a groan that was almost a curse. The figures were still there.

He suddenly rose to his feet and gave himself a shake. He determined to go to his club; he would find company there,—perhaps not the best, but it would be better than this awful loneliness and deadly silence.

He went through the hall softly, almost stealthily; put on his hat and coat; let himself quietly out of the door and stepped forth into the night.

It had stopped snowing and the stars looked down from a clearing sky. The moon just

above the housetops was sailing along a burn-
ished track. The vehicles went slowly by with
a muffled sound broken only by the creaking
of the wheels in the frosty night. From the
cross streets, sounded in the distance the jan-
gle of sleigh-bells.

CHAPTER IX

LIVINGSTONE plodded along through the snow, relieved to find that the effort made him forget himself and banished those wretched figures. He traversed the intervening streets and before he was conscious of it was standing in the hall of the brilliantly lighted club. The lights dazzled him, and he was only half sensible of the score of servants that surrounded him with vague, half-proffers of aid in removing his overcoat.

Without taking off his coat, Livingstone walked on into the large assembly-room to see who might be there. It was as empty as a church. The lights were all turned on full and the fires burned brightly in the big hearths; but there was not a soul in the room, usually so crowded at this hour.

Livingstone turned and crossed the marble-paved hall to another spacious suite of rooms. Not a soul was there. The rooms were swept and garnished, the silence and loneliness seeming only intensified by the brilliant light and empty magnificence.

Livingstone felt like a man in a dream from which he could not awake. He turned and made his way back to the outer door. As he did so he caught sight of a single figure at the far end of one of the big rooms. It looked like Wright,—the husband of Mrs. Wright to whom Livingstone had sent his charity-subscription a few hours before. He had on his overcoat and must have just come in. He was standing by the great fire-place rubbing his hands with satisfaction. As Livingstone turned away, he thought he heard his name called, but he dashed out into the night. He could not stand Wright just then.

He plunged back through the snow and once more let himself in at his own door. It was lonelier within than before. The hall was ghastly. The big rooms, bigger than they had ever seemed, were like a desert. It was intolerable! He would go to bed.

He slowly climbed the stairs. The great clock on the landing stared at him as he passed and in deep tones tolled the hour—of ten. It was impossible! Livingstone knew it must have been hours since he left his office. To him it seemed months, years;—but his own watch marked the same hour.

As he entered his bedroom, two pictures hanging on the wall caught his eye. They were portraits of a gentleman and a lady. Any one would have known at a glance that they were Livingstone's father and mother. They had hung there since Livingstone built his house, but he had not thought of them in years. Perhaps, that was why they were still there.

They were early works of one who had

since become a master. Livingstone remembered the day his father had given the order to the young artist.

"Why do you do that?" some one had asked. " He perhaps has parts, but he is a young man and wholly unknown."

" That is the very reason I do it," had said his father. " Those who are known need no assistance. Help young men, for thereby some have helped angels unawares."

It had come true. The unknown artist had become famous, and these early portraits were now worth—no, not those figures which suddenly gleamed before Livingstone's eyes!—

Livingstone remembered the letter that the artist had written his father, tendering him aid when he learned of his father's reverses —he had said he owed his life to him—and his father's reply, that he needed no aid, and it was sufficient recompense to know that one he had helped remembered a friend.

[97]

Livingstone walked up and scanned the portrait nearest him. He had not really looked at it in years. He had had no idea how fine it was. How well it portrayed him! There was the same calm forehead, noble in its breadth; the same deep, serene, blue eyes;—the artist had caught their kindly expression;—the same gentle mouth with its pleasant humor lurking at the corners;—the artist had almost put upon the canvas the mobile play of the lips;—the same finely cut chin with its well marked cleft. It was the very man.

Livingstone had had no idea how hand-some a man his father was. He remembered Henry Trelane saying he wished he were an artist to paint his father, but that only Van Dyck could have made him as distinguished as he was.

He turned to the portrait of his mother. It was a beautiful face and a gracious. He re-membered that every one except his father

[98]

SANTA CLAUS'S PARTNER

had said it was a fine portrait, but his father
had said it was, "only a fine picture; no portrait of her could be fine."

Moved by the recollection, Livingstone
opened a drawer and took from a box the
daguerreotype of a boy. He held it in his hand
and looked first at it and then at the portraits
on the wall. Yes, it was distinctly like both.
He remembered it used to be said that he was
like his father; but his father had always said
he was like his mother. He could now see the
resemblance. There were, even in the round,
unformed, boyish face, the same wide open
eyes; the same expression of the mouth, as
though a smile were close at hand ; the same
smooth, placid brow. His chin was a little
bolder than his father's. Livingstone was
pleased to note it.

He determined to have his portrait painted
by the best painter he could find. He would
not consider the cost. Why should he ? He

[99]

SANTA CLAUS'S PARTNER

was worth—at the thought the seven gleaming figures flashed out clear between his eyes and the portrait in his hand.

Livingstone turned suddenly and faced himself in the full length mirror at his side. The light caught him exactly and he stood and looked himself full in the face. What he saw horrified him. He felt his heart sink and saw the pallor settle deeper over his face. His hair was almost white. He was wrinkled. His eyes were small and sharp and cold. His mouth was drawn and hard. His cheeks were seamed and set like flint. He was a hard, wan, ugly old man; and as he gazed, unexpectedly in the mirror before his eyes, flashed those cursed figures.

With almost a cry Livingstone turned and looked at the portraits on the wall. He half feared the sharp figures would appear branded across those faces. But no, thank God! the figures had disappeared. The two faces beamed down on him sweet and serene and comforting as heaven.

Under an impulse of relief Livingstone flung himself face downward on the bed and slipped to his knees. The position and the association it brought fetched to his lips words which he used to utter in that presence long years ago.

It had been long since Livingstone had prayed. He attended church, but if he had any heart it had not been there. Now this prayer came instinctively. It was simple and childish enough : the words that he had been taught at his mother's knee. He hardly knew he had said them ; yet they soothed him and gave him comfort; and from some far-off time came the saying, " *Except ye become as little children, ye shall not enter—*" and he went on repeating the words.

Another verse drifted into his mind : " *And he took a child and set him in the midst of them, and said, * * * Whosoever shall humble him-*

[101]

self as this little child, the same is greatest. And whoso shall receive one such little child in my name receiveth me. But whoso shall offend one of these little ones which believe in me, it were better for him that a millstone were hanged about his neck, and that he were drowned in the depth of the sea."

The events of the evening rose up before Livingstone — the little girl in her red jacket, with her tear-stained face, darting a look of hate at him; the rosy-cheeked boys shouting with glee on the hillside, stopped in the midst of their fun, and changing suddenly to yell their cries of hate at him; the shivering beggar asking for work, — for but five cents, which he had withheld from him.

Livingstone shuddered. Had he done these things? Could it be possible? Into his memory came from somewhere afar off: "*Inasmuch as ye have done it unto one of the least of these my brethren, ye have done it unto me.*"

[102]

There flashed through his mind the thought, might he not retrieve himself? Was it too late? Could he not do something for some one?— perhaps, for some little ones?

It was like a flash of light and Livingstone was conscious of a thrill of joy at the idea, but it faded out leaving him in blanker darkness than before. He did not know a single child. — He knew in a vague, impersonal way a number of children whom he had had a momentary glimpse of occasionally at the fashionable houses which he visited; but he knew them only as he would have known handsomely dressed dolls in show windows. He had never thought of them as children, but only as a part of the personal belongings of his acquaintances—much as he thought of their bric-à-brac or their poodles. They were not like the children he had once known. He had never seen them romp and play or heard them laugh or shout.

[103]

He was sunk in deep darkness.

In his gloom he glanced up. His father's serene face was beaming down on him. A speech he had heard his father make long, long ago, came back to him: "Always be kind to children. Grown people may forget kindness, but children will remember it. They forgive, but never forget either a kindness or an injury."

Another speech of his father's came floating to Livingstone across the years: "If you have made an enemy of a child, make him your friend if it takes a year! A child's enmity is never incurred except by injustice or meanness."

Livingstone could not but think of Clark's little girl. Might she not help him? She would know children. But would she help him?

If she were like Clark, he reasoned, she would be kind-hearted. Besides, he remembered to have heard his father say that chil-

SANTA CLAUS'S PARTNER

dren did not bear malice : that was a growth of older minds. It was strange for Livingstone to find himself recurring to his father for knowledge of human nature — his father whom he had always considered the most ignorant of men as to knowledge of the world.

He sprang to his feet and looked at his watch. Perhaps, it was not yet too late to see the little girl to-night if he hurried? Clark lived not very far off, in a little side street, and they would sit up late Christmas Eve.

As he turned to the mirror it was with trepidation, his last glance at it had been so dreadful ; but he was relieved to find a pleasanter expression on his face. He almost saw a slight resemblance to his father.

The next moment he hurried from the room ; stole down the stair ; slipped on his overcoat, and hastily let himself out of the door.

CHAPTER X

IT was quite clear out now and the moon was riding high in a cloudless heaven. The jingle of sleigh-bells had increased and just as Livingstone turned the corner a sleigh dashed past him. He heard the merry voices of young people, and amid the voices the ringing laughter of a young girl, clear as a silver bell.

Livingstone stopped short in his tracks and listened. He had not heard anything so musical in years—he had not heard a young girl's laughter in years—he had not had time to think of such things. It brought back across the snow-covered fields—across the snow-covered years—a Christmas of long ago when he had heard a young girl's musical laughter like a silvery chime, and, standing there in the snow-covered street, for one moment Livingstone was young again - no longer a gray-

haired man in the city; but a young man in
the country, somewhere under great arching
boughs; face to face with one who was also
young;—and, looking out from a hood that
surrounded it like a halo, a girlish face flashed
on him: cheeks like roses, brilliant with the
frosty air; roguish eyes, now dancing, now
melting; a laughing mouth from which came
such rippling music that there was no simile
for it in all the realm of silvery sound, the
enchanting music of the joy of youth.

With a cry, Livingstone sprang forward
with outstretched, eager hands to catch the
vision; but his arms enclosed only vacancy
and he stood alone in the empty street.

A large sleigh came by and Livingstone
hailed it. It was a livery vehicle and the driver
having just put down at their homes a party
of pleasure-seekers was on his way back to
his stable. He agreed with Livingstone to
take him to his destination and wait for him,

and Livingstone, giving him a number, sprang in and ordered him to drive rapidly.

The sleigh stopped in front of a little house, in a narrow street filled with little houses, and Livingstone getting out mounted the small flight of steps. Inside, pandemonium seemed to have broken loose somewhere up-stairs, such running and shouting and shrieks of joyous laughter Livingstone heard. Then, as he could not find the bell, Livingstone knocked.

At the sound the noise suddenly ceased, but the next moment it burst forth again louder than before. This time the shouts came rolling down the stairs and towards the door, with a scamper of little feet and shrieks of childish delight. They were interrupted and restrained by a quiet, kindly voice which Livingstone recognized as Clark's. The father was trying to keep the children back.

It might be Santa Claus himself, Livingstone heard him urge, and if they did not go back to bed immediately, or into the back room,—or even if they peeped, Santa Claus might jump into his sleigh and drive away and leave nobody at the door but a grocer's boy with a parcel. This direful threat had its effect. The gleeful squeals were hushed down into subdued and half-awed murmurs and after a little a single footstep came along the passage and the front door was opened cautiously.

At sight of Livingstone, Clark started, and by the light of the lamp the caller could see his face pale a little. He asked Livingstone in with a voice that almost faltered. Leaving Livingstone in the little passage for a moment Clark entered the first room—the front room —and Livingstone could hear him sending the occupants into a rear room. He heard the communicating door close softly. Every sound was suddenly hushed. It was like the sudden hush of birds when a hawk appears. Livingstone thought of it and a pang shot through him. Then the door was opened and Clark somewhat stiffly invited Livingstone in.

The room was a small front parlor.

The furniture was old and worn, but it was not mean. A few old pieces gave the room, small as it was, almost an air of distinction. Several old prints hung on the walls, a couple of portraits in pink crayon, such as St. Mimin used to paint, and a few photographs in frames, most of them of children,— but among them one of Livingstone himself.

All this Livingstone took in as he entered. The room was in a state of confusion, and a lounge on one side, with its pillows still bearing the imprint of an occupant, showed that the house held an invalid. In one corner a Christmas-tree, half dressed, explained the litter. It was not a very large tree; certainly it was not very richly dressed. The things that hung on it were very simple.

Many of them evidently were of home-manu-
facture—knots of ribbon, little garments, sec-
ond-hand books, even home-made toys.

A small pile of similar articles lay on the
floor, where they had been placed ready for
service and had been left by the tree-dressers
on their hasty departure.

Clark's eye followed instinctively that of
the visitor.

" My wife has been dressing a tree for the
children," he said simply.

He faced Livingstone and offered him a
chair. He stiffened as he did so. He was evidently prepared for the worst.

Livingstone sat down. It was an awkward
moment. Livingstone broke the ice.

" Mr. Clark, I have come to ask you a favor
—a great favor—"

Clark's eyes opened wide and his lips even
parted slightly in his astonishment.

"— I want you to lend me your little girl—

the little girl I saw in the office this afternoon."

Clark's expression was so puzzled that Livingstone thought he had not understood him.

"'The Princess with the Golden Locks,'" he explained.

"Mr. Livingstone!—I—I den't understand." He looked dazed.

Livingstone broke out suddenly: "Clark, I have been a brute, a cursed brute!"

"Oh! Mr. Liv—!"

With a gesture of sharp dissent Livingstone cut him short.

"It is no use to deny it, Clark.—I have—I have!—I have been a brute for years and I have just awakened to the fact!" He spoke in bitter, impatient accusation. "I have been a brute for years and I have just realized it."

The face of the other had softened.

"Oh, no, Mr. Livingstone, not that. You have always been just—and—just;" he protested kindly. "You have always—"

—"Been a brute," insisted Livingstone, "a blind, cursed, selfish, thoughtless—"

"You are not well, Mr. Livingstone," urged Clark, looking greatly disturbed. "Your servant, James, said you were not well this evening when I called. I wanted to go in to see you, but he would not permit me. He said that you had given positive orders that you would not see—"

"I was not well," assented Livingstone. "I was suffering from blindness. But I am better, Clark, better. I can see now—a little."

He controlled himself and spoke quietly. "I want you to lend me your little girl for—" He broke off suddenly. "How many children have you, Clark?" he asked, gently.

"Eight," said the old clerk. "But I have n't one I could spare, Mr. Livingstone."

"Only for a little while, Clark?" urged the other; "only for a little while.—Wait, and let me tell you what I want with her and why I

[113]

want her, and you will — For a little while?" he pleaded.

He started and told his story and Clark sat and listened, at first with a set face, then with a wondering face, and then with a face deeply moved, as Livingstone, under his warming sympathy, opened his heart to him as a dying man might to his last confessor.

"—And now will you lend her to me, Clark, for just a little while to-night and to-morrow?" he pleaded in conclusion.

Clark rose to his feet. "I will see what I can do with her, Mr. Livingstone," he said, gravely. "She is not very friendly to you, I am sorry to say — I don't know why."

Livingstone thought he knew.

"Of course, you would not want me to compel her to go with you?"

"Of course not," said Livingstone.

CHAPTER XI

THE father went out by the door that opened into the passage, and the next moment Livingstone could hear him in deep conference in the adjoining room; at first with his wife, and then with the little girl herself.

The door did not fit very closely and the partition was thin, so that Livingstone could not help hearing what was said, and even when he could shut out the words he could not help knowing from the tones what was going on.

The mother was readily won over, but when the little girl was consulted she flatly refused. Her father undertook to coax her.

To Livingstone's surprise the argument he used was not that Livingstone was rich, but that he was so poor and lonely; not well off and happy like him, with a house full

[115]

of little children to love him and make him happy and give him a merry Christmas.

The point of view was new to Livingstone — at least, it was recent; but he recognized its force and listened hopefully. The child's reply dashed his hopes.

"But, papa, I hate him so — I just *hate* him!" she declared, earnestly. "I'm *glad* he hasn't any little children to love him. When he wouldn't let you come home to us this evening, I just prayed so hard to God not to let him have any home and not to let him have any Christmas — not *ever!*"

The eager little voice had risen in the child's earnestness and it pierced through the door and struck Livingstone like an arrow. There came back to him that sentence, *"Whoso offendeth one of these little ones, it were better for him that a millstone were hanged about his neck —."*

[116]

Livingstone fairly shivered, but he had able defenders.

"Oh, Kitty!" exclaimed both her father and mother, aghast at the child's bitterness.

They next tried the argument that Livingstone had been so kind to the father. He had "given him last year fifty dollars besides his salary."

Livingstone was not surprised that this argument did not prove as availing with the child as the parents appeared to expect.— Fifty dollars! He hated himself for it. He felt that he would give fifty thousand to drop that millstone from his neck.

They next tried the argument that Livingstone wanted to have a Christmas-tree for poor children and needed her help. He wanted her to go with him to a toy-shop. He did not know what to get and wished her to tell him. He had his sleigh to take her.

This seemed to strike one of the other

members of the family, for suddenly a boy's eager voice burst in :

"I'll go with him. I'll go with him in a sleigh. I'll go to the toy-shop. Maybe, he'll give me a sled. Papa, mamma, please let me go."

This offer, however, did not appear to meet all the requisites of the occasion and Master Tom was speedily suppressed by his parents. Perhaps, however, his offer had some effect on Kitty, for she finally assented and said she would go, and Livingstone could hear the parents getting her ready. He felt like a reprieved prisoner.

After a few moments Mr. Clark brought the little girl in, cloaked and hooded and ready to go.

When Livingstone faced the two blue eyes that were fastened on him in calm, and, by no means, wholly approving inspection, he felt like a deep-dyed culprit. Had he known of

SANTA CLAUS'S PARTNER

this ordeal in advance he could not have faced it, but as it was he must now carry it through.

What he did was, perhaps, the best that any one could have done. After the cool, little handshake she vouchsafed him, Livingstone, finding that he could not stand the scrutiny of those quiet, unblenching eyes, threw himself on the child's mercy.

" Kitty," he said earnestly, " I did you this evening a great wrong, and your father a great wrong, and I have come here to ask you to forgive me. — I have been working so hard that I did not know it was Christmas, and I interfered with your father's Christmas — and with your Christmas ; for I had no little girls to tell me how near Christmas was. And now I want to get up a Christmas for some poor children, and I don't know how to do it, so I have come to ask you to help me. I want you to play Santa Claus for me, and we will

[119]

find the toys, and then we will find the children. I have a great big sleigh, and we will go off to a toy-shop, and presently I will bring you back home again."

He had made his speech much longer than he had intended, because he saw that the child's mind was working; the cumulative weight of the sleigh-ride, the opportunity to play a part and to act as Santa Claus for other children, was telling on her.

When he ended, Kitty reflected a moment and then said quietly, " All right."

Her tone was not very enthusiastic, but it was assent and Livingstone felt as though he had just been redeemed.

The next moment the child turned to the door.

Livingstone rose and followed her. He was amused at his feeling of helplessness and dependence. She was suddenly the leader and without her he felt lost.

SANTA CLAUS'S PARTNER

She stepped into the sleigh and he followed her.

"Where shall we go first?" she asked.

This was a poser for Livingstone. All the shops of which he knew anything were closed long ago.

"Why, I think I will let you select the place," he began, simply seeking for time.

"What do you want to get?" she asked calmly, gazing up at him.

Livingstone had never thought for a second that there would be any difficulty about this. He was hopelessly in the dark. Stocks, "common" or "preferred," bonds and debentures, floated through his mind. Even horses or pictures he would have had a clear opinion on, but in this field he was lost. He had never known, or cared to know, what children liked.

Suddenly a whole new realm seemed to open before him, but it was shrouded in darkness. And that little figure at his side with

[121]

large, sober, searching eyes fixed calmly on him was quietly demanding his knowledge and waiting for his answer. He had passed hundreds of windows crowded with Christmas presents that very evening and had never looked at one. He had passed as between blank walls. What would he not have given now for but the least memory of one glance!

But the eyes were waiting and he must answer.

"Why—ah—you know,—ah—*toys!*"

It was an inspiration and Livingstone shook himself with self-approval.

"Yes—ah—TOYS! you know?" he repeated. He glowed with satisfaction over his escape.

The announcement, however, did not appear to astonish his companion as much as he felt it should have done. She did not even take her eyes from his face.

"How many children are there?"

"Why—twenty." Livingston caught at a number, as a sinking man catches at a twig.

As she accepted this, Livingstone was conscious of elation. He felt as though he were playing a game and had escaped the ignominy of a wrong answer: he had caught a bough and it held him.

"How old are they?"

Livingstone gasped. The little ogress! Was she just trifling with him? Could it be possible that she saw through him? As he looked down at her the eyes fastened on him were as calm as a dove's eyes.

"Why—ah—. How many brothers and sisters have you?" he asked.

He wished to create a diversion and gain time. She answered promptly.

"Seven: four sisters and three brothers. John, he's my oldest brother; Tom, he's next —he's eight. Billy is the baby."

This contribution of family history was a

[123]

relief, and Livingstone was just trying to think of something else to say, when she demanded again,

"What are the ages of your children?"

"I have no children," said Livingstone, thinking how clever he was to be so ready with an answer.

"I know. — But I mean the children you want the toys for?"

Livingstone felt for his handkerchief. The perspiration was beginning to come on his brow.

"Why, — ah — the same ages as your brothers and sisters — about," he said desperately, feeling that he was at the end of his resources and would be discovered by the next question.

"We will go to Brown's," said the child quietly, and, dropping her eyes, she settled herself back in the furs as though the problem were definitely solved.

HE TOOK THE SHOPKEEPER ASIDE AND HAD A LITTLE
TALK WITH HIM.

CHAPTER XII

LIVINGSTONE glanced at the little figure beside him, hoping she would indicate where "Brown's" was, but she did not. Every one must know "Brown's."

The only "Brown" Livingstone knew was the great banker, and a grim smile flickered on his cheek at the thought of the toys in which that Brown dealt. He shifted the responsibility to the driver.

"Driver, go to Brown's. You know where it is?"

"Well, no, sir, I don't believe I do. Which Brown do you mean, sir?"

"Why—ah—the toy-man's, of course."

The driver stopped his horses and reflected. He shook his head slowly. Livingstone, however, was now equal to the emergency. Besides, there was nothing else to do. He turned to his companion.

"Where is it?" he began boldly, but as he saw the look of surprise in the little girl's face he added, "I mean — exactly?"

"Why, right across from the grocer's with the parrot and the little white woolly dog."

She spoke with astonishment that any one should not know so important a personage. And Livingstone, too, was suddenly conscious of the importance of this information. Clearly he had neglected certain valuable branches of knowledge.

Happily, the driver came to his rescue.

"Where is that, Miss?" he asked.

"You go to the right and keep going to the right all the way," she said definitely.

Livingstone was in despair; but the driver appeared to understand now.

"You tell me when I go wrong," he said, and drove on.

He must have children at home, thought Livingstone to himself as the sleigh after a

number of turns drew up in front of one of
the very windows Livingstone had passed that
evening on the back street. He felt as though
he would like to reward the driver. It was the
first time Livingstone had thought of a driver
in many years.

Just as they drove up the door of the shop
was being closed, and the little girl gave an
exclamation of disappointment.

"Oh, we are too late!" she cried.

Livingstone felt his heart jump into his
throat. He sprang to the door and rapped.
There was no answer. The light was evidently
being turned off inside. Livingstone rapped
again more impatiently. Another light was
turned down. Livingstone was desperate. His
loud knocking produced no impression, and
he could have bought out the whole square!

Suddenly a little figure pushed against him
as Kitty slipped before him, and putting her
mouth to the crack of the door, called,

"Oh! Mr. Brown, please let me in. It's *me*, Kitty Clark, Mr. Clark's little girl."

Instantly the light within was turned up. A step came towards the door, the bolts were drawn back and half the door was opened.

Livingstone was prepared to see the shop-keeper confounded when he should discover who his caller was. On the contrary, the man was in nowise embarrassed by his appearance. Indeed, he paid no attention whatever to Livingstone. It was to Kitty that he addressed himself, ignoring Livingstone's presence utterly.

"Why, Kitty, what are you doing out at this time of night? Aren't you afraid Santa Claus will come while you are away, and not bring you anything? You know what they say he does if he don't find everybody asleep in bed?"

Kitty nodded, and leaning forward on her

toes, dropped her voice to a mysterious whisper :

" I know who Santa Claus is." The whisper ended with a little chuckle of delight at her astuteness. " I found it out last Christmas."

" Kitty, you did n't ! You must have been mistaken ? " said the shopkeeper with a grin on his kindly countenance. " Who is he ?"

" Mr. — Brown, and Mr. and Mrs. — Clark," said Kitty slowly and impressively, as though she were adding up figures and the result would speak for itself. She took in the shop with a wave of her little hand and a sweep of her eyes.

" I 'm playing Santa Claus myself, to-night," she said, tossing her hooded head, her eyes kindling at the thought. The next look around was one of business.

" This is Mr. Livingstone, papa's employer." She indicated that gentleman.

Mr. Brown held out his plump and not wholly immaculate hand.

[129]

"How d'ye do, sir? I think I've heard of you?"

He turned back to Kitty.

"Who for?" he asked.

"For him," Kitty nodded. "He's got a whole lot of little children—not his own children—other people's children—that he's going to give Christmas presents to, and I've come to help him. What have you got left, Mr. Santa Claus?"

She stood on tiptoe and peered over the shelves.

"Well, not a great deal, Miss Wide-awake," said the shopkeeper dropping into her manner and mood. "You see there's lots of children around this year as don't keep wide-awake all night, and Santa Claus has had to look after 'em quite considerable. I can't tell you how many sleighs full of things he's taken away from this here very shop. He didn't leave nothing but them things you see and the very expensive things in the cases. He said they were too high-priced for him."

He actually gave Livingstone a wink, and Livingstone actually felt flattered by it.

The reply recalled Kitty to her business. She turned to Mr. Livingstone.

"How much money have you got to spend?" she asked.

"Umhm—I don't know," said Livingstone.

"As much as a dollar?"

"Yes."

"More?"

"Yes."

"How much more?"

"As much as you want. Suppose you pick out the things you like and then we can see about the price," he suggested.

"Some things cost a heap."

She was looking at a doll on whose skirt was pinned a little scrap of card-board marked, "*25c*."

"Yes, they do," assented Livingstone. "But they are worth it," he thought. "I tell you what!—Suppose you look around and see just what you like, and I'll go off here and talk with Mr. Brown so as not to disturb you."

He was learning and the lesson was already bringing him pleasure.

He took the shopkeeper aside and had a little talk with him, learning from him all he could of Clark's family and circumstances. It was an amazement to him. He had never known what a burden Clark had carried. The shopkeeper spoke of him with great affection and with great respect.

"He is the best man in the world," he said.

He treated Livingstone with familiarity, but he spoke of Clark with respect.

"He ought to be on the Avenue," he asserted; "and if everybody had their rights some would be where Mr. Clark is and Mr. Clark would be in their place."

Livingstone was not prepared just then to gainsay this.

He explained to Mr. Brown his wishes. He wanted to get many things, but did not know how to keep the child from suspecting his plan. The shopkeeper gave him a suggestion. Close association and sympathy with children had given Brown knowledge.

CHAPTER XIII

THEY returned to Kitty. She was busy figuring on a little piece of paper, moistening her little stub of a pencil, every other second, with her tongue. Her little red mouth showed streaks of black. She was evidently in some trouble.

Livingstone drew near.

"How are you coming on?" he asked.

She looked up with a face full of perplexity.

"Oh! I've spent nearly the whole dollar and I haven't but nine presents yet. We must get something cheaper. — But they were so pretty!" she lamented, her eyes glancing longingly towards the articles she had selected.

"Let's see. Maybe, you have made a mistake," said Livingstone. He took the bit of paper and she handed him the pencil.

"I'm not very good at making figures," she observed.

SANTA CLAUS'S PARTNER

"I'm not either," said Livingstone, glancing at the paper. "I'll tell you what let's do," he said. "Let's get Mr. Brown to open all his cases and boxes, and let's look at everything and just see what we would select if we could have our choice?"

The little girl's eyes opened wide.

"You mean, let's make pretense that we are real sure-enough Santa Claus and just pick out everything we want to give everybody, and pretend that we could get it and give it to them?"

Livingstone nodded.

"Yes."

That was just what he ought to have meant, he knew.

The inquiry in Kitty's big eyes became light. She sprang to her feet and with a little squeak of delight marched to the middle of the shop and taking her stand began to sweep the shelves with her dancing eyes.

[135]

Livingstone gave a nod to the shopkeeper and he drew back the curtains that protected the cases where the finer and more expensive goods were kept and began to open the boxes.

Kitty approached on tiptoe and watched him with breathless silence as though she were in a dream which a word might break.

Then when she had seen everything she turned back to Livingstone.

"Well!" she said slowly.

"Well, what do you say?" He too was beginning to feel a spell.

"Well, if I were a real, sure-'nough Santa Claus, I'd just get—everything in those cases." The spread of her little arms took it all in.

"And what would you do with it?" asked Livingstone in the same low tone, fearful of breaking the reverie in which she stood wrapped.

He had never before in all his life been

taken into partnership by a little girl, and deep down beneath his breast-pocket was a kindling glow which was warming him through and through.

"I'd carry that doll—to Jean, and that— to Sue, and that—to Mollie, and that—to Dee, and those skates to Johnny, and—that sled to Tom, and—that woolly lamb to little Billy, 'cause he loves squshy things.—And then —I'd take all the rest in my sleigh and I'd go to the hospital where the poor little children have n't got any good papas and mammas like me to give them anything, and where Santa Claus can't ever go, and I'd put something by the side of every bed—of every one, and, maybe, they'd think at first it was only a dream; but when they waked up wide they'd find Santa Claus had been there, sure enough!"

In her energy she was gesticulating with earnest hands that seemed to take each pre-

sent and bear it to its destination, and she
concluded with a little nod to Livingstone
that seemed to recognize him as in sympathy
with her, and to say, "Would n't we if we only
could?"

It seemed to Livingstone as though a casing
of ice in which he had been enclosed had suddenly broken and he were bathed in warmth.

The millstone round his neck had suddenly
dropped and he shot upward into the light.

The child was leading him into a new and
vernal world. He wanted to take her in his
arms and press her to his heart. The differ-
ence between the glance she now gave him
and that she had shot at him at the door of
his office that evening came to him and decided him. It was worth it all.

"Yes. Is there anything else you wish?" he
asked, hoping that there might be, for she had
not mentioned herself.

"Yes, but it's not anything Santa Claus can

give," she said calmly; "I have asked God for it."

"What?" asked Livingstone.

"Something to make mamma well: to help papa pay for the house. He says it's that 'at keeps her ill, and she says if she were well he could pay for it: and I just pray to God for it every day."

Livingstone caught his breath quickly as if from a sudden pain. The long years of Clark's faithful service flashed before him. He shivered at the thought of his own meanness. He was afraid those great eyes might see into his heart. He almost shrivelled at the thought.

"Well, let's take a sleigh-ride and see if any other shops are open. Then we can return."

He spoke a few words aside to Mr. Brown. The shopkeeper's eyes opened wide.

"But you say you haven't money enough with you, and I don't know you?"

Livingstone smiled.

[139]

"Why, man, I am worth—" He stopped short as a faint trace of seven figures appeared vaguely before his eyes. "I am worth enough to buy all this square and not feel it," he said, quickly correcting himself.

"That may be all so, but I don't know you," persisted the shopkeeper. "Do you know anybody in this part of the town?"

"Well, I know Mr. Clark. He would vouch for me, but—."

The shopkeeper turned to the child.

"Kitty, you know this gentleman, you say?"

"Yes. Oh, he's all right," said Kitty decisively. "He's my papa's employer and he gave him *fifty* dollars last Christmas, 'cause my papa told me so."

This munificent gift did not appear to impress Mr. Brown very much, any more than it did Livingstone, who felt himself flush.

"Business is business, you know?" said the shopkeeper,—an aphorism on which Livingstone had often acted, but had never had cited against him.

The shopkeeper was evidently considering. Livingstone was half angry and half embarrassed. He felt as he had not done in twenty years. The shopkeeper was weighing him in his scales as he might have done a pound of merchandise, and Livingstone could not tell what he would decide. There was Kitty, however, her eyes still filled with light. He could not disappoint her. She, too, felt that he was being weighed and suddenly came to his rescue.

"He's an awful kind man," she said earnestly. "He hasn't got any little children of his own, and he's going to give things to little poor children. He always does that, I guess," she added.

"Well, no, I don't," said Livingstone, looking at the shopkeeper frankly; "but I wish I had, and I'll pay you."

"All right. She knows you and that will do," said Mr. Brown.

Kitty, with the light of an explorer in her eyes, was making new discoveries on the shelves, and the two men walked to the back of the shop where the shopkeeper wrote a list of names. Then Livingstone and Kitty got into the sleigh and drove for a half-hour or so.

On their return Mr. Brown was ready.

His shop looked as though it had been struck by a whirlwind. The floor and counters were covered with boxes and bundles, and he and Livingstone packed the big sleigh as full as it would hold, leaving only one seat deep in the furs amid the heaped up parcels. Then suddenly from somewhere Mr. Brown produced a great, shaggy cape with a hood, and Livingstone threw it around Kitty and getting in lifted her into the little nest between the furs.

Kitty's eyes were dancing and her breath was coming quickly with excitement.

It was a supreme moment.

"Where are we going, Mr. Livingstone?" she whispered. She was afraid to speak aloud lest she might break the spell and awake.

"Just where you like."

"To the Children's Hospital," she panted.

"To the Children's Hospital, driver," repeated Livingstone.

Kitty gave another gasp.

"We'll play you're Santa Claus," she said, in a voice of low delight.

"No. Play you are Santa Claus's partner," said Livingstone.

"And you?"

"You are not to say anything about me."

CHAPTER XIV

LIVINGSTONE had not had such a drive in years. The little form snuggled against him closer and closer and the warm half sentences of childish prattle, as the little girl's imagination wove its fancies, came to him from amid the furs and made him feel as though he had left the earth and were driving in a new world. It was like a dream. Had youth come back? Was it possible?

The sleigh stopped in front of a great long building.

"You have to ring at the side door at night," said the driver. He appeared to know a good deal about the hospital.

Livingstone sprang out and rang the bell and then stepped back.

"When they open the door, you are to do all the talking," he said to Kitty as he lifted her down.

THE LITTLE FORM SNUGGLED AGAINST HIM CLOSER AND CLOSER.

"Who shall I say rang?" she asked.

"Santa Claus's partner."

"But you —?"

"No. You are not to mention my name. Remember!"

Before the child could reply the door opened a little way and a porter looked out.

"Who's there?" he called to the sleigh, rather overlooking the little figure in the snow.

"Santa Claus's partner," said Kitty.

"What do you want?" He peered out at the sleigh. He was evidently sleepy and a little puzzled. "We don't take in anything at this hour except patients." He looked as if he were about to shut the door when a woman's voice was heard within speaking to him and the next moment the door was opened wide and he gave way as a matronly figure came forward and stood in the archway.

"Who is it?" she asked in a very pleasant

[145]

voice, looking down at the little figure in the snow before her.

"Santa Claus's partner," said Kitty, gazing up at her.

"What do you want, dear?" The voice was even pleasanter.

"To leave some presents for the children."

"What children?"

"All the good children—all the sick children, I mean—all the children," said Kitty.

The matron turned and spoke to the porter, showing to Livingstone, as she did so, a glimpse of a finely cut profile and a comely figure silhouetted against the light within. The bolts were drawn from the gate of the driveway and the doors rolled back.

"Come in," said the matron, and the little figure enveloped in the shaggy cape and hood walked in under the big arch followed by the sleigh, whilst Livingstone withdrew a short distance into the shadow.

It was some time before the doors opened again and Kitty reappeared, but Livingstone did not mind it. It was cold too, but neither did he mind that. He was warm. As he walked up and down in the empty street before the long building his heart was warmed with a glow which had not been there for many and many a long year. He was not alone. Once more the memory of other Christmases passed through his mind in long processional, but now not stamped with irretrievable opportunity, to mock him with vain regret for lost happiness; only tinged with a sadness for lost friends who came trooping about him; yet lightened by his resolve to begin from now on and strive as best he might to retrieve his wasted life, and whilst he bore his punishment do what he could to make atonement for his past.

Just then across the town the clocks began to sound the midnight hour, and as they

[147]

ceased, from somewhere far-away church bells mellowed by the distance began to chime the old Christmas hymn : —

" While shepherds watched their flocks by night,
All seated on the ground,
The angel of the Lord came down,
And glory shone around."

Livingstone stood still to listen, in a half-dream.

Suddenly before him in the snow stood a little figure muffled in a shaggy cape with hood half thrown back. The childish face was uplifted in the moonlight. With lips half parted she too was listening, and for a moment Livingstone could hardly take in that she was real. She seemed —!

Could she be — ?

" The angel of the Lord came down," —chimed the mellow bells.

The chiming died out.

"Christ is born," said the child. "You heard the bells?"

"Yes," said Livingstone humbly.

"It's all done," she said; "and I prayed so hard that not one of them stirred, and now when they wake they'll think it was real Santa Claus. They say he always comes at twelve and I counted the clocks.—I wonder if he went home?" She was speaking now to herself; but Livingstone answered.

"I'm sure of it," he said.

"*The angel of the Lord came down,*" still chimed in his ears.

Suddenly a little warm hand was slipped into his confidingly.

"I think we'd better go home now." The voice was full of deep content.

Livingstone's hand closed on hers and as he said "Yes," he was conscious of a pang at the thought of giving her up.

He lifted her to put her in the sleigh. As

SANTA CLAUS'S PARTNER

he did so the little arms were put about his neck and warm little lips kissed him. Livingstone pressed her to his breast convulsively and climbed into the sleigh without putting her down.

Neither spoke and when the sleigh stopped in front of Mr. Clark's door the child was still in Livingstone's arms, her head resting on his shoulder, the golden curls falling over his sleeve. Even when he transferred her to her father's arms she did not wake. She only sighed with sweet content and as Livingstone bent over and kissed her softly, muttered a few words about "Santa Claus's partner."

A half-hour later, Livingstone, after another interview with Mr. Brown who was awaiting him patiently, drove back again to Mr. Clark's door with another sleighful of packages which were all duly transferred to the small room where stood the little Christmas-tree.

The handshake Livingstone gave John

SANTA CLAUS'S PARTNER

Clark as he came down the steps of the little house was the warmest he had given any man in twenty years. It was so warm that it seemed to send the blood tingling through Livingstone's heart and warm it anew.

CHAPTER XV

LIVINGSTONE drove home through silent streets, but they were not silent for him. In his ears a chime was still ringing and it bore him far across the snow-filled streets and the snow-filled years to a land of warmth and light. The glow was still about his heart and the tingle which the pressure of Kitty Clark's arms about his neck, and John Clark's clasp of his hand had started still kept it warm.

At his door Livingstone dismissed his driver and as he cheerily wished him a merry Christmas the man's cheery reply showed that Livingstone had already found the secret of good cheer.

"The same to you, your honor; the same to you, sir," said the driver heartily, as he buttoned up his pocket with a pat of satisfaction. "We 've had a good time to-night, sir, have n't we? And I wish you many more like it, sir. And when Christmas comes along next time I hope you'll remember me, for I'll remember you; I've had a little child in that 'ere same horspital. God took her to Himself twelve years ago. They're good to 'em there, rich and poor all alike;—and 't is n't every night I can drive 'Santa Claus's partner.'"

Livingstone stood and watched the sleigh till it drove out of sight. Even after it had disappeared around a corner, he still listened to the bells. It seemed to him he had a friend in it.

Livingstone let himself in noiselessly at his door, but the softness with which he turned the key this time was to keep from disturbing his servants, not to keep them from seeing him.

He stopped stock still on the threshold. The whole house seemed transformed. The hall was a bower of holly and mistletoe, and

[153]

SANTA CLAUS'S PARTNER

the library, as Livingstone entered it, with its
bright fire roaring in the hearth and its festoons and wreaths, seemed once more a charm-
ing home: a bower where cheer might yet
make its abode.

As quietly, however, as Livingstone had entered, his butler had heard him.

As Livingstone turned to take in all the
beauty of the room, James was standing before
him. His face showed some concern, and his
voice, as he spoke, had a little tremor in it.

"When we found you had gone out, sir, we
were afraid you might be sick, and the cook
has got something hot for you?"

Livingstone glanced about to find a phrase
with which to thank him for the trouble they
had taken; but the butler spared him the
pains.

"We thought we would try to make the
house look a little cheery, sir. Hope you don't
mind, sir?"

[154]

"Mind!" said Livingstone, "I am delighted; and I thank you very much. Mind? I should think not!"

The tone of his voice and the light in his eye showed that there was a change in him and it acted like a tonic on the butler. The light came into his eyes too. He drew a breath of deep relief as though a mountain of care had rolled off him, and he came a step nearer his master, who had flung himself into a chair and picked up a cigar.

The next minute Livingstone plunged into the subject on his mind. It was a plan which made the butler's eyes first open wide and then sparkle with pleasure.

The difficulty with Livingstone, however, was that the next day was a holiday and he did not know whether what he wanted could be got.

The butler came to his rescue. It was no difficulty to James. Such an emergency only

[155]

quickened his powers. He knew places where whatever was wanted could be got, holiday or no holiday, and, "If Mr. Livingstone would only allow him—?"

"Allow you!" said Livingstone, "I give you *carte blanche*, only have everything ready by five o'clock.—Ask the cook to send up whatever she has; I'm hungry, and we'll talk it over whilst I'm taking supper."

"Yes, sir; yes, sir; yes, sir;" and James withdrew with a step as light as air.

"Extraordinary servant!" thought Livingstone. "Wonder I never took it in before!"

Ten minutes later Livingstone was seated at the table with an appetite like a schoolboy's.

It was the happiest meal Livingstone had eaten in many a long day; for, all alone as he was, he was not alone. Thought-of-others sat at the board and a cheery companion it is.

"Tell the laundress to be sure and bring her children around to-morrow, and be sure you make them have a good time," he said to James, as he rose from the table. James bowed.

"Yes, sir."

"And ascertain where policeman, No. 268, is to be found to-morrow. I want to send a contribution to make a good slide for some boys on his beat."

James bowed again, his eyes somewhat wider than before.

As Livingstone mounted the stair, though he was sensible of fatigue it was the fatigue of the body, so delicious to those who have known that of the mind. And he felt pity as well as loathing for the poor, worn creature who had climbed the same stair a few hours before.

As he entered his room the warmth and home feeling had come back there also. The portraits of his father and mother first caught his eye. Some one had put a wreath around each and they seemed to beam on him with a pleased and tender smile. They opened afresh the flood-gates of memory for him, but the memories were sweet and tender.

He glanced at a mirror almost with trembling. The last time he had looked at himself he had seen only that old, haggard face with the ghostly figures branded across the brow. Thank God! they were gone now, and he could even see in his face some faint resemblance to the portraits on the wall.

He went to bed and slept as he had not slept for months, perhaps for years—not dreamlessly, but the dreams were pleasant. —Now and then lines of vague figures appeared to him, but a little girl with a smiling face came and played bo-peep with him over them, and presently sprang up and threw her arms about his neck and made him take her in a sleigh to a wonderful shop where they could get marvellous presents; among them

Youth, and Friendship, and Happiness. The door was just being shut as they arrived, but when he called his father's name it was opened wide—and his father and mother greeted him—and led him smiling into places where he had played as a child.—And Catherine Trelane in a shaggy coat and hood pulled the presents from a forest of Christmas-trees and gave them to Santa Claus's partner to give to others. And suddenly his father, with his old tender smile, picked the little girl up in his arms and she changed into a wonderful child that shone so that it dazzled Livingstone and—he waked to find the bright sun shining in through the window and falling on his face.

He sprang from bed with a cry almost of joy so bright was the day; and as he looked out of the window on the sparkling snow out-side it seemed a new world.

CHAPTER XVI

ALL the morning Livingstone "rushed" as he had never "rushed" in the wildest excitement of "the street." He had to find a banker and a lawyer and a policeman. But he found them all. He had to get presents to Sipkins and Hartly and the other clerks; but he managed to do it.

His servants, too, had caught the contagion, and more than once big wagons driven by smiling, cheery-faced men drove up to the door and unloaded their contents. And when the evening fell and a great sleigh with six seats and four horses, and every seat packed full, drove up and emptied its shouting occupants out at Livingstone's door everything was ready.

It was Livingstone himself who met the guests at the door, and the driver, in his shaggy coat, must have been an old friend from the smiling way in which he nodded and waved his fur-gloved hands to him, as he helped Mrs. Clark out tenderly and took Kitty into his arms.

When Kitty was informed that this was Santa Claus's Partner's party, and that she was to be the hostess, she was at first a little shy, partly, perhaps, on account of the strangeness of being in such a big, fine house, and partly on account of the solemn presence of James, until the latter had relieved her in ways of which that austere person seemed to have the secret where children were concerned. Finally she was induced to take the children over the house, and the laughter which soon came floating back from distant rooms showed that the ice was broken.

Only two rooms, the library and the dining-room, were closed, and they were not closed very long.

Just as it grew dark Kitty was told to marshal her eager forces and James with sparkling eyes rolled back the folding doors.

[161]

SANTA CLAUS'S PARTNER

The children had never seen anything before in all their lives like that which greeted their eyes. The library was a bower of evergreen and radiance. In the centre was a great tree of crystal and stars which reflected the light of a myriad twinkling candles. It had undoubtedly come from fairy-land, if the place was not fairy-land itself, on the border of which they stood amazed.

Kitty was asked by Mr. Livingstone to lead the other children in, and as she approached the tree she found facing her a large envelope addressed to,

Santa Claus's Partner, Miss Kitty Clark.

This she was told to open and in it was a letter from Santa Claus himself.

It stated that the night before, as the writer was engaged in looking after presents for some poor children, he saw a little girl in a shop engaged in the same work, and when he reached

AND JAMES, WITH SPARKLING EYES, ROLLED BACK THE FOLDING-DOORS.

a certain hospital he found that she had been there, too, before him, and now as he had to go to another part of the world to keep ahead of the sun, he hoped that she would still act for him and look after his business here.

The letter was signed,

Your partner, Santa Claus.

The postscript suggested that a few of the articles he had left on the tree for her were marked with names, but that others were unmarked, so that her friends might choose what they preferred, and he had left his pack at the foot of the tree as a grab-bag.

This letter broke the spell and next moment every one was shouting and rollicking as though they lived there.

In all the throng there was no one so delighted as Mr. Clark. Livingstone had had no idea how clever he was. He was the soul of the entertainment. It was he who discovered

[163]

first the packages for each little one; he who, without appearing to do so, guided them in their march around the tree, so that all might find just the presents that suited them. He seemed to Livingstone's quickened eye to divine just what each child liked and wished. He appeared to know all that Livingstone desired to know.

At length, he alone of all the guests had received no present. The others had their little arms packed so full that Livingstone had to step forward to the tree to help a small tot bear away his toppling load.

The next moment Kitty discovered a large envelope lying at the foot of the tree. It was addressed,

John Clark, Esq.,
Father of Santa Claus's Partner.

It was strange that Kitty should have overlooked it before.

[164]

With a spring she seized it and handed it to her father with a little shout of joy, for she had not been able to keep from showing disappointment that he had received nothing.

Clark smiled at her pleasure, for he knew that the kisses which she had given him from time to time had been to make amends to him, and not, as others thought, from joy over her own presents.

Clark knew well the hand-writing, and even as he opened the envelope he glanced around to catch Livingstone's eye and thank him. Livingstone, however, had suddenly disappeared; so Clark read the letter.

It was very brief. It said that Livingstone had never known until the night before how much he owed him; that he was not sure even now that he knew the full extent of his indebtedness, but at least he had come to recognize that he owed much of his business success to Mr. Clark's wisdom and fidelity;

and he asked as a personal favor to him that Clark would accept the enclosed as a token of his gratitude, and would consider favorably his proposal.

Opening an enclosed envelope, Clark found two papers. One was a full release of the mortgage on Clark's house (Livingstone had spent the morning in securing it), the other was a Memorandum of "Articles of Partnership" between Berryman Livingstone and John Clark, beginning from that very day, -indeed, from the day before,—all ready, signed by Livingstone and wanting only Mr. Clark's signature to make it complete.

Mr. Clark, with his face quite white and looking almost awed, turned and walked into the next room where he found Livingstone standing alone. The old clerk was still holding the papers clutched in his hand and was walking as if in a dream.

" Mr. Livingstone," he began, " I can never

—I am overwhelmed!—Your letter—your gifts—" But Livingstone interrupted him. His face was not white but red.

"Nonsense!" he said, as he turned and put his hand on the other's shoulder. "Clark, I am not giving you anything. I am paying.— I mean, I owe you everything, and what I don't owe you, I owe Kitty. Last night you lent me—" He stopped, caught himself, and began again.

"It was more than even you knew, Clark," he said, looking the other kindly in the eyes, "and I'll owe you a debt of gratitude all my life. All I ask is, that you will forget the past and help me in the future and sometimes lend me Kitty. I never knew until now how good it was to have a partner."

Just then he became conscious that someone else was near him. Kitty, with wide-open, happy eyes, was standing beside them looking up inquiringly in their faces. The child seemed

[167]

to know that something important had happened, for she put up her arms, and pulling her father down to her kissed him, and then turning quickly she caught Livingstone and, drawing him down, kissed him too.

"I love you," she said, in a whisper.

Livingstone caught her in his arms.

"Let's go and have a game of blind-man's buff. I am beginning to feel young again," he said, and linking his arm in Clark's, he dragged him back to the others, where, in a few minutes they were all of one age, and a very riot of fun seemed to have broken loose.

Matters had just reached this delightful point, and Livingstone was down on his hands and knees trying with futile dexterity to avoid the clutch of a pair of little arms that apparently were pursuing him with infallible instinct into an inextricable trap, when he became conscious of a presence he had not observed before. Some one not there before was standing in the doorway.

Livingstone sprang to his feet and faced Mrs. Wright.

He felt very red and foolish as he caught her eyes and found them smiling at him. The idea of being discovered in so ridiculous a situation and posture by the most fashionable and elegant woman of his acquaintance! But Mrs. Wright waved to him to go on with his game and the next moment the little arms had clutched him, and, tearing off her bandage, Kitty, with dancing eyes, declared him " caught."

"Well, this is my final triumph over Will," exclaimed Mrs. Wright, advancing into the room, as Livingstone, drawing the little girl along with him, approached her. And she began to tell Livingstone how they had particularly wanted him to dine with them that day as an old friend of his had promised to come to them, but they had supposed, of course, that he had been overrun with invitations for the day and, as they had not seen him of late, thought that he had probably gone out of town, until her husband saw him at the club the night before where he had gone to find some poor lone bachelor who might have no other invitation.

"You know Will has always been very fond of you," she said; "and he says you have been working too hard of late and have not been looking well. When I did n't get my usual contributions from you this Christmas I did n't know what to make of it, but I think that on my round this morning I have found out the reason?"

Livingstone knew the reason, but he did not tell her. The knowing smile that lit her face, however, mystified him and he flushed a little under her searching eyes.

"Will was sure he saw you in the club last

night," she persisted, "and he tried to catch you, but you ran off; and now I have come for you and will take no refusal."

Livingstone expressed his regret that he could not come. A wave of his hand towards the curly heads and beaming faces clustered before them and towards the long table gleaming in the dining-room beyond explained his reason.

"I am having a Christmas dinner myself," he said.

"Then you will come in after they go?" insisted Mrs. Wright, and as Livingstone knew they were going early he assented.

"Who are your friends?" she asked. "What a pleasant-looking man, and what lovely children! That little girl,—I thought it was Cupid when she had the bandage on her eyes and now I am sure of it."

"Let me present them to you," said Livingstone, and he presented Mr. Clark as his partner and Kitty as Santa Claus's partner.

SANTA CLAUS'S PARTNER

"I did not know you had a partner?" she asked.

"It is my Christmas gift from Santa Claus," he said. " One of them ; I have many."

CHAPTER XVII

WHEN Livingstone walked into Mrs. Wright's drawing-room that evening he had never had such a greeting, and he had never been in such spirits. His own Christmas dinner had been the success of his life. He could still see those happy faces about his board, and hear those joyous voices echoing through his house.

The day seemed to have been one long dream of delight. From the moment when he had turned to go after the little child to ask her to show him the way to help others, he had walked in a new land; lived in a new world; breathed a new air; been warmed by a new sun.

Wright himself met him with a cordiality so new to Livingstone and yet so natural and unforced that Livingstone wondered whether he could have been living in a dream all these years or whether he was in a dream to-night.

Among the guests he suddenly came on one who made him think to-night must be the dream.

Mrs. Wright, with glowing eyes, presented him to a lady dressed in black, as "an old friend, she believed:" a fair, sweet-looking woman with soft eyes and a calm mouth.

The name Mrs. Wright mentioned was "Mrs. Shepherd," but as Livingstone looked the face was that of Catherine Trelane.

The evening was a fitting ending to a happy day—the first Livingstone had had in many a year. Even Mrs. Shepherd's failure to give him the opportunity he sought to talk with her could not wholly mar it.

Later, Livingstone heard. Mrs. Wright begin to tell some one of his act of the night before, in buying up a toy-shop for the children at the hospital.

"I always believed in him," she asserted warmly.

Livingstone caught his name and, turning to Mrs. Wright, with some embarrassment and much warmth, declared that she was mistaken, that he had not done it.

Mrs. Wright laughed incredulously.

" I suspected it this morning when I first heard of it; but now I have the indisputable proof."

She held up a note.

"'I think I 've heard of you before,'" she laughed, with a capital imitation of Mr. Brown's manner.

"I still deny it," insisted Livingstone, blushing, and as Mrs. Wright still affirmed her belief, he told her the story of Santa Claus's partner.

Insensibly, as he told it, the other voices hushed down.

He told it well; for his heart was full of the little girl who had led him from the frozen land back to the land of light.

[175]

SANTA CLAUS'S PARTNER

As he ended, from another room somewhere up-stairs, came a child's clear voice sing-
ing,

God rest you, mer-ry gentle-men,
Let nossing you dismay ;
For Jesus Christ our Sa-viour
Was born this ve-ry day.

Livingstone looked at Mrs. Shepherd.

She was standing under the long evergreen
festoons just where they met and formed a
sort of verdant archway. Two of the children
of the house, attracted by Livingstone's story,
had come and pressed against her as they
listened with interested faces, and she had
put her arms about them and drawn their
curly heads close to her side. A spray of holly
with scarlet berries was at her throat and
one of the children had mischievously stuck a
sprig of mistletoe in her hair. Her face was
turned aside, her eyes were downcast, the

[176]

STANDING, IN THE CHRISTMAS EVENING LIGHT, IN A LONG
AVENUE UNDER SWAYING BOUGHS.

SANTA CLAUS'S PARTNER

long, dark lashes drooping against her cheek, and on her face rested a divine compassion; and as Livingstone gazed on her he saw the same gracious figure and fine profile that he had seen the night before outlined against the light in the archway of the gate of the Children's Hospital. It was the reflective face of one who has felt; but when she raised her eyes they were the eyes of Catherine Trelane. And suddenly, as Livingstone looked into them, they had softened, and she seemed to be standing, as she had stood so long ago, in the Christmas evening light in a long avenue under swaying boughs, in the heart of the land of his youth.

While still, somewhere above, the child's voice carolled,

> —*Let nossing you dismay ;*
> *For Jesus Chwist our Sa-wiour*
> *Was born this ve-wy day.*

FINIS

D. B. Updike
The Merrymount Press
Chestnut Street
Boston

www.ingramcontent.com/pod-product-compliance
Lightning Source LLC
Chambersburg PA
CBHW030835270326
41928CB00007B/1056